HAPPY CLOUD EXPLOITATION NATION

MR BRUNELLE EXPLAINS IT ALL	2
DOWN THE RABBIT HOLE	3
LISA PETRUCCI KEEPING SOMETHING WEIRD ALIVE	4
WE'RE STILL STANDING	16
HAPPY CLOUD MEDIA, LLC	16
DREAMHAVEN BOOKS AND COMICS	19
RHONDA #APPRECIATION	20
ANDRAS #GRATITUDE	21
HORROR REALM	22
CINEMA WASTELAND	23
STEW MILLER	24
DOUG WALTZ	27
NATHAN RUMLER	29
THE MUMMY AND THE MONKEY	30
EXPLOIT THIS!	33
SPEAKING CONFIDENTIALLY, OR, REFLECTING KACMARYNSKI	35
JASON MCDANIEL	37
SEAN DONOHUE	39
TIM RITTER	40
TOM DEVLIN AND TOM DEVLIN'S MONSTER MUSEUM	44
ROSS SNYDER	45
2021: TRAVEL PREPARED TO SURVIVE	47
ART LINKLETTER HEARTILY ENDORSES AUTHOR JAMES SABATA	48
TIM GROSS	50
TOM BERDINSKI	52
WILLIAM ADCOCK	54
DON ENGLAND	56
MISTI BONDY	57
JEFF MONAHAN	65
ROCKY ROAD TO THE CINEPOCALYPSE	68
SHADOWS AND LIGHT	75
NOTLD 90: THE VERSION YOU'VE NEVER SEEN	76
NIGHTMARE PAVILLION	77
THE FINAL INTERVIEW	78
BLOODSUCKER CITY AUTHOR INTERVIEW:	79
GAUNTLET PRESS	81
HEADPRESS	82
I'D BUY THAT FOR A DOLLAR!	83
IT'S (PROBABLY) NOT A SEQUEL TO LESS THAN ZERO	89

Exploitation Nation
is published by
Happy Cloud Media, LLC
Vol. 1, No. 12 © 2021

Amy Lynn Best:
Publisher

Mike Watt:
Editor-in-Chief

Ally Melling:
Editor

Carolyn Haushalter:
Asst. Editor

Gianna Leonne:
Transcription

Robert Waldo Brunelle:
Moral Compass

Art Director:
Ryan Hose

Cover:
Stew Miller

Special Thanks to:
Lisa Petrucci
Vinegar Syndrome
and all the contributors
to this special issue.

All photographic and artistic content copyright the original holders and is included here for promotional purposes only. No rights are implicit or implied.

Exploitation Nation is published periodically by Happy Cloud Media, LLC (Amy Lynn Best and Mike Watt, PO Box 816, Venetia, PA 15367). Exploitation Nation Issue #12 (ISBN 978-1-951036-24-9) is © 2021 by Happy Cloud Media, LLC. All rights reserved. All featured articles and illustrations are copyright 2021 by their respective writers and artists. Reproductions of any material in whole or in part without its creator's written permission is strictly forbidden. Exploitation Nation accepts no responsibility for unsolicited manuscripts, DVDs, stills, art, or any other materials. Contributions are accepted on an invitational basis only.
Visit Us At www.exploitation-nation.com, Facebook.Com/ExploitationNation, and www.happycloudpublishing.com

DOWN THE RABBIT HOLE

"We're still standing." That was meant to be the theme of this issue. "2020 tried to kill us all, but we, the undersigned, are still here. Despite the economy, the pandemic, the massive bouts of depression and insanity we all suffered, we're still here. We're still making art. We're still writing and filming and creating. And here's the proof." We'd hoped to have more contributors.

The biggest problem Indie creators suffer is lack of self-esteem. We're not, for the most part, expert marketing gurus. We have trouble promoting ourselves. Others, no problem. Ourselves? Aw, shucks, you don't want to hear about us.

It was tough to keep a schedule this year. Not just for *Exploitation Nation*, either. We heard from other publishers and distributors that things just wouldn't adhere to a reasonable timeline. The universe refused to co-operate. The nice thing about hearing about other peoples' failures is it puts your own into perspective.

The fact remains: the folks here are good folks putting out some amazing and marvelous stuff. We have actors, writers, traditional artists, tattoo artists, directors, sculptors, a couple of conventions you'll want to check out if you're masked and vaxxed. Check out their sites. Order stuff. One dollar in the Indie community goes around three times and makes more art. Disney uses your money to dry its tears of joy.

In other news, our "sister magazine," *Grindhouse Purgatory*, is celebrated its twentieth and final issue this past October. It'll be quite the collector's issue, so snatch it up while you can. Next year, it will rise from the ashes as a new *Descent into Hell* under the banner *Grindhouse Inferno*, focusing more on reviews and essays on classic exploitation cinema from folks who lived it and risked their lives to see it! *G.I.* is looser and more profane than *E.N.*, but will still live up to the high journalistic standards you've come to rely on, only with more swearing. Look for *G.I.* to launch around March, 2022.

As for *E.N.* and Happy Cloud Media, LLC, we have new books in the works, restoration on our classic films is finally underway and you'll have even more opportunities to check us out!

So there, 2021! Ya kicked us all around the best you could. See you in 2022.

— Mike Watt, August, 2021.

LISA PETRUCCI KEEPING SOMETHING WEIRD ALIVE

by Mike Watt

If you're reading this, I don't need to tell you who Lisa Petrucci is, or what *Something Weird Video* does. (And if you're not reading this, then I'm talking to myself and we have bigger problems.) The Short Answer: *Something Weird Video* was begun in 1990 by filmophile and Patron Saint of Sleaze Preservation, Mike Vraney, collecting thousands of movies and preserving the cultural heritage of such exploitation luminaries as David F. Friedman, Herschell Gordon Lewis, Doris Wishman, Harry Novak, and dozens of unsung, unknown heroes of the roughies, the nudie cuties, the soft-core, and even the hardcore porn worlds that proliferated on 42nd Street in Manhattan. When Mike passed in 2014, his widow and partner continued doing what they'd always done.

During the pandemic, Lisa almost single-handedly packed 10,000 orders for dedicated *Something Weird* fans worldwide. If anything fits the standard of "still standing," it's *Something Weird* and its ethos to keep the weirdest of our history alive.

What follows is a conversation we had just as the light of day dawned this past summer...

SWV'S Lisa Petrucci. (All photos this section courtesy and copyright Lisa Petrucci.)

Lisa: Oh, I don't know if they were 10,000 discs, but they were a lot. Everybody else was trying to figure out what to do during the pandemic—not me. I was working 60 hours a week. What happened was in January of 2020—it was literally January 1st or 2nd—I made this public announcement that we were gonna be ending the DVDR part of our catalog, or most of it, I should say. We are keeping quite a lot of them. And that people would have 1 year to be able to order whatever ones they want. Now, I'll preface this with the fact that sales were in the toilet. Nobody was buying DVDRs for years. At least the last five years we were not making any revenue from that source. We had consistent orders, but they were, like, people ordering two or three. I'd be maybe making 50 a week. That's not enough to keep a person employed as the manufacturing. And also all of our machines are getting older, and I didn't want to upgrade everything and buy all new machines, and then you're using new media. At the same time as well our old machines were starting to crap-out, and it was getting harder to get the disks that work in those machines. So there was just all of these signs from the universe that it was time...

Mike: To put an end to this?

Lisa: Right. I gotta keep reminding people this, because any time I hear a customer whine about this decision, I tell them, "If Mike Vraney was still alive, *Something Weird* would've shut down about five years ago." Because he was done, even before he got sick. He was like, "We're gonna go out and do something else." Just because of the direction that everything was going in, and we were moving towards digital and streaming and other things like that. But then the pandemic happened. I did start getting a lot of orders right away in January, then the pandemic, and then I think a lot of people had either extra spare time or they were getting that enhanced unemployment benefits and stuff, but orders were great. Then

Producer David F. Friedman, Lisa, and Mal Arnold, Blood Feast's own Fuad Ramses.

in December it was a nightmare. Literally the last two weeks of December there were so many orders coming in it was making me sick to my stomach. Cause I'm like, "How am I gonna fulfill these?"

Mike: It's not so much success when you're buried under it.

Lisa: No, it's not. And also when you've got two people doing all of the work, cause I wanted to give everybody their opportunity to get what they needed, but I actually had to tell some customers cause their orders were gonna be too big that, uh, no. You just can't. I'm gonna have to limit the number because it would've been just impossible for us to do a 600 order piece for one person. It took until June of 2021 to make all of the orders from the last week of December. And I ended up telling a lot of our customers, "Oh, could you wait until 2021? We'll do this manually. Make your list, and I'll get back to you."

So we have been doing that as well, but since my vacation things are back to normal. It's slooooow, and that's OK with me.

Mike: What would be astonishing to me when outside of our circle is how well this stuff endures, because *Something Weird's* catalog is so heavy on these orphaned or unwanted children. Loops of things. You're preserving stuff that most people would have thrown away in some cases. And you consider everything a bit of film history no matter what it is, and that was always something I admired. Why is this stuff still enduring? I ask Frank [Henenlotter] this all the time, and he gives me different answers.

Lisa: I think for many, it a nostalgic thing. Maybe some saw a particular film when they were younger, at a drive-in or grindhouse, but also now there's a younger audience and those who are just discovering *SWV* for the first time—a whole new generation of genre film fans out there who are seeing these films for the first time. Many of our older or elderly customers only order via snail mail or phone and don't use the internet. Unfortunately, many are pretty bummed out that we pulled the plug on most of the DVD-Rs. However, most titles are still available to download, so it's not like you can't watch them. Personally, I just don't want to make DVD-Rs for the rest of my life. I need to move on to do other more creative projects.

Mike: It's fascinating to me because I got to meet a lot of the legends towards the end of their lives. I was lucky enough to do that, with Doris and Herschell and Dave Friedman. These were nice, hardworking people. Herschell always played down his films. Doris would make up these wonderful lies. I'd be writing for a half-hour and she'd be like, "Oh, that was all a lie!" [Laughs] For better or worse, whatever the term is, they were creating their own styles, their own methods of doing things.

Lisa: All those folks made significant contributions to sexploitation and exploitation cinema. We were fortunate that they were still around in the '90s and early 2000's when you could actually meet and talk to the legends who produced, directed and distributed those films. There's so few of them left.

Lisa with the marvelous Doris Wishman.

That was one of the reasons that Mike Vraney was ready to wind things down before he got sick. After most of his beloved cronies passed away he would say, "It's just not as fun anymore."

And in our little world, the only exploiteer who's left that I deal with on a regular basis (and love to pieces) is Bill Grefé (*Sting of Death, Death Curse of Tartu*). He's in his early nineties and recently had his films restored and re-released in a beautiful Blu-ray collection through Arrow Films.

Like Dave Friedman would always say about the exploitation film business: "It's like a sack of flour. Just keep shaking it and a little more comes out." These movies continue to make money decades after their original theatrical runs—as second and third features, then on VHS, then DVD and now Blu-ray and streaming. There's a lot of life left in those low budget films, for sure.

Mike: And you've made it easier because before *Something Weird*, and I'm sure you've encountered this as well, you had to go into some sketchy places to find this stuff. I'm sure went Mike into some bizarre places to gather all the materials. You preserved the griminess.

Lisa: I embrace that. Even with so many changing attitudes culturally, I'm not going to change the way we've always done and presented the *SWV* catalog. Mike's motto was to be as abrasive as possible and push the envelope. Mike went to adult movie theatres (since the time he could grow a mustache) and thoroughly enjoyed his vintage porn, so he was a consumer as well as a preservationist. He loved old smut.

Mike: It's funny. You're both the most pleasant people in the world to meet. I've mentioned both over the years a couple of times. We're talking stuff we love, and the dichotomy is so much of this stuff is based on violence and sex because it's all exploitation. You're exploiting these elements, and I guess the journalist in me wants to sit down and say, "As a woman how do you …?" But I know you get it.

Lisa: With so many people coming down on what they consider to be "problematic" content, I view these films as time capsules that deserve to exist. In the early '90s when I started doing research on sixties sexploitation cinema, what interested me most was the starlets in these films and the women who were involved in the adult film industry, like Doris Wishman and Roberta Findlay. I saw this as a very feminist action (even though both Doris and Roberta denied being feminists themselves.) Being an actress in an adult motion picture was unusual since most women back then had very traditional jobs and roles—many were mothers, wives, teachers, secretaries, nurses or other very societally acceptable professions. To decide to be an actress in a nudie movie was very brave. But in retrospect, many women have relied on sex work as a way to support themselves for centuries, and I respect that.

In the sexploitation film world, everyone loved working with Dave Friedman. He was a pro. The guy cut his teeth at Paramount and working with legendary Kroger Babb. Friedman had a long history in the film business even before he started producing his own films. In particular, he treated his actresses very well, unlike some of the creeps you often hear stories about.

Mike: What was your journey to this world of sex and violence and misogyny and bizarre nature?

Lisa: Oh gosh. I've liked horror movies since I was a kid and used to go to the drive-in with my mother. She and her boyfriend (my parents were divorced) would put me in the backseat and take me to the drive-in with them. I was exposed to so many totally inappropriate movies for a kid, like *Night of the Living Dead* and *The Corpse Grinders*. And then I just gravitated to those kinds of films in my late teens and twenties. Back then you could watch weird movies on basic cable. There were some pretty great networks like USA and others that were showing films like *Werewolves on Wheels* and *Psychomania* right on television. That re-introduction to drive-in type movies made me realize I was seriously interested in and thoroughly enjoyed exploitation films.

I have a background in art history with a film studies minor, so I began to go down the rabbit hole of cult films from the '50s to the '70s. I wanted to see as many as humanly possible, but in the early to mid-1980s it was still pretty limited as to what was out there on home video. I'd go to any offbeat film screenings, in fact I used to do film programming at a college, so I'd rent a lot 16mm films from Kit Parker, mostly because I wanted to watch them. By the late '80s and early '90s I was juggling working at art galleries, making my own art, and writing about fringe popular culture. I lived in NYC about two blocks from Kim's Video. All it took was me walking into Kim's for the first time, and *oh my gawd*. Anything and everything I'd ever want to watch was there. That was basically like going to community college for smut.

I started renting all the Russ Meyer movies and the "big box" VHS tapes that were available at the time. Lo and behold, one day I see these really brightly colored VHS clam cases with titles like *The Sin Syndicate, Bad Girls Go to Hell* and *Diary of a Swinger*. I didn't know what those films were, but thought I should definitely check them out. That was the beginning of my entering the world of *Something Weird Video*. During that time, I also worked at Michael Weldon's Psychotronic Store in the East Village. There were a lot of *Something Weird* videos on the shelves for sale and Mike Vraney's name came up many times because he consigned VHS tapes and movie memorabilia at the store.

Mike Vraney used to set up at the Chiller Theatre conventions in New Jersey. He was very close friends with the promoter, Kevin Clement, for decades. I used to go to Chiller as fan girl, and one day heard that Dave Friedman was going to be a guest. I had recently read his autobiography *A Youth in Babylon*, and thought I should get in touch with *SWV*. I called the office and talked to Mike, who I had never spoken to before, and I said, "Hey, I'm gonna be coming to Chiller. Can I interview you and Dave Friedman?" And that was the fateful day that my life changed forever, when I met Mike.

Mike: But you already had the education by the time you met him. It wasn't like you were a wide-eyed fangirl. You knew what you were talking about by the time you got in there.

Lisa: It was funny because Mike asked me, "What movies do you like?" And I responded, "Oh, I really love the films of Doris Wishman and the Findlays." His eyes lit up and he said "Wow!" I guess he had never heard a woman say that before. We became fast friends, and had a long distance relationship since he was in Seattle and I was still living in NYC. I wrote a few pieces about sexploitation cinema for various magazines, and Mike would send me advance screeners of any new *SWV* releases to review. It was super fun getting to see these films before anyone else, Those were very special days, but eventually our relationship developed into more than being just friends and fans of smutty movies. I moved to the West Coast in 1994, originally to Los Angeles, but after three months of being there, the Northridge earthquake happened and I didn't want to live there anymore. By then, Mike asked me to move to Seattle to be with him and work for *SWV*. At the time I wasn't too sure, but in retrospect it was the best decision I ever made in my life.

Mike: And after Mike passed, you still kept the mantle going, even long after, as you mentioned, he was thinking of changing gears.

Lisa: I've been involved with *SWV* since 1994. Mike passed away in January 2014. So for over twenty years *SWV* has been my life, besides being an artist. I was able to do both during the time Mike and I were together. It was an on again off again schedule where if I knew that if I had an art exhibition coming up I'd be focused on painting. But when I wasn't making art, I'd be helping Mike by doing research, writing reviews, and also designing catalogs and video cases. So, by the time of his death, *SWV* was just as much a part of my life as it was his. During the last few months of Mike's life we had some really tough conversations. He said, "I don't want you to be stuck with this (meaning *SWV*). You need to move on with your life and do what makes you happy."

But what he didn't realize is that this is a huge part of my life, as well as the fact that it was very important to me to honor his legacy and hard work. The reason I keep this going is mostly because of him. He didn't care about preserving his own legacy, so it's all up to me. Obviously I derive an income from *SWV* as well as getting to work on fun projects that I can put my own stamp on. But in the end it's about Mike, the man was gung-ho about genre films, and he put so much time and effort into finding these lost classics. I couldn't just let *SWV* go without me overseeing things and making sure that his legacy is honored properly. Which is why I work so closely with the partners—like AGFA, Severin Films, Kino Lorber, The Film Detective, Pop Cinema and others—who are restoring and re-releasing SWV classics on Blu-ray and streaming nowadays.

Mike: I feel like kind of a jerk for even asking the question now. With all of that in mind, why do you think it needs to be preserved?

Lisa: I think when Mike first started finding original film elements in the 1990s he realized that there must be hundreds, maybe thousands more out there. Up until then, Mike was basically a bootlegger (like pretty much everyone else was in those days), taking existing content recorded from television or dubbed from other legitimate VHS tapes and selling it collector-to-collector. He was just a fan like the rest of us and excited when he discovered that he could record VHS tapes, sell them, and put food on the table for his kids. Then around 1991-92 he came into a large collection of girlie, classic striptease and wrestling women 8mm & 16mm loops and realized that none of it had really been available on home video before. He got the films transferred locally, they were pretty low quality scans, and put out the first compilations of *Nudie Cuties, Grindhouse Follies,* and *Wrasslin' She Babes.* They sold like gangbusters and it made him realize that he needed to find more. Then he got access to his first collection of 35mm sexploitation films. Mike wasn't a film archivist when he started collecting original film elements, but from then on was excited to unearth as many of these bottom-of-the-barrel obscurities as he could and share them with the world. Mike was living the dream and never had a real job in his whole life. The man lived by his own rules.

He didn't transfer those 35mm films right away. What he did was, while working as a projectionist at the Apple Theatre in Seattle, sometimes he'd screen some of his 35mm films instead of the usual porno movies. Customers were probably wondering what the hell they were watching, expecting to see *Pretty Peaches* or whatever the hell was normally on rotation and instead *The Sin Syndicate* is on the screen. What he would do is take a camcorder and shoot the screen so that he had the 35mm film on a video! Which was hilarious because as he's shooting the video there are people walking in front of the camera! It was those DIY videos of the 35mm films being screened at the Apple Theatre that were first official sexploitation VHS releases.

Mike put ads in *Big Reel* magazine and some other film collector forums. But the turning point was when he heard from David F. Friedman. Friedman heard that SWV was selling his *The Ribald Tales of Robin Hood*—which Mike pirated from a VHS tape—and called the office one day and said to Mike, "Hey! You're selling my movie without my permission!" and Mike responded, "Yeah! People love it!" They met up in Las Vegas (Friedman was at a showmen's convention there) to discuss the possibility of legitimately licensing films. They hit it off and Friedman invited Mike to his film vault on Cordova Street where he still had his archive in storage and Friedman asked, "Well, what are you interested in?"

Mike said, "I want all of it." They agreed to start with just a few key titles, then Mike saw a can labeled *Space Thing*, and asked "What's this?"

And Dave says, "That's the worst science fiction movie ever made!" And Mike responds, "I want it!" At that point Mike took around a half dozen films out of vault and had them transferred in Los Angeles and that's when *SWV* did the first official Dave Friedman releases. When Dave got his first royalty check he was so shocked. After that, Dave said, "Kid, you can have it all!"

From that point forward, Dave introduced Mike to many of his cronies—including Harry Novak, Bob Cresse, and Arthur Morowitz of Distribpix. Funny thing though, *SWV* was already selling a few Herschell Gordon Lewis and Doris Wishman titles on VHS which were from pre-existing tape sources. Jimmy Maslon, who owns both those libraries, called SWV very much the same way Dave did, and asked what the hell was going on. Within an hour Mike and Jimmy were pals and had a made a licensing deal for both Herschell and Doris' films. I swear, someday I will write a book. There's so many stories to tell!

Lisa and Mike Vraney.

Mike: Do you have a favorite Doris story?

Lisa: Of course. Over the years, I had talked to Doris on the phone, but the first time I actually met her was in Boston. She was live in person at a screening of *Bad Girls Go to Hell* organized by Michael Bowen. So I went to Boston to visit family and go to the screening, but The Cramps were also playing that same night, so I decided to do both. There was a blizzard that evening, and there's sweet little Doris standing there in a pair of open-toed high heel mules, with a foot of snow outside. She was wearing a cute little jacket with a leopard fur color. It was so awesome to finally meet her and we chit-chatted for awhile. Of course she was wearing her trademark dark sunglasses, but when she took them off for just a minute some guy snapped a photo really fast and she exclaimed, "You monster!" and totally laid into him. It was priceless. Anyway, that was fun and I've heard some great stories from Jimmy Maslon about Doris and how his deal with her transpired. She is my hero. I wake up every morning and ask myself, "What would Doris Wishman do?" and act accordingly.

Mike: I couldn't imagine answering that question. Do you wanna talk about Herschell for a minute?

Lisa: Sure. I was aware of Herschell's films from the time I was little because kids in the schoolyard used to talk about *Blood Feast*. I don't know if any of them had actually seen it, but the film was notorious back then. During the 1980s I saw many of the HG Lewis films on home video. In fact, *Color Me Blood Red* was a big inspiration for a painting series that I

With the gregarious Herschell Gordon Lewis.

did. Around the time I started working for SWV, Herschell became a big part of our lives. We would often have Herschell and Jimmy as our guests at conventions. I often tell people that I think I spent more time with Dave, Bill, and Herschell than I did my own father, which is kinda weird if you think about it.

Herschell was always really great to have at a convention because he totally wowed the crowds. I used to say, "Just wind him up and let him go!" He'd tell the same stories over and over, but no one got tired of them, including me. He'd treat each fan like they were special, and was genuinely appreciative of fandom and generously gave them his time. One thing I loved about him and Dave was that they weren't at the conventions to shake down the rubes. Dave just wanted to sign autographs and give them away. I'd have to remind him that the conventions had rules and that he had to charge them something even if it was just a dollar. Fans loved coming to the *SWV* table because they could sit and hang out with these legends, whereas many other celebrities were more mercenary and stingy with their time, "Give me your money, take a photo, and get the hell out of here."

Usually if we had Dave and Herschell in town for something, there were always the three hour dinners at fancy restaurants that we'd have to endure because at their age those guys lived to eat. We'd hear stories about the old days, especially if you plied Dave with booze. Herschell didn't drink, but was relaxed enough to share stories that most had never heard before. Mike and I spent a month in Scandinavia with Dave (and that's a book right there!) So many crazy things happened over the course of the tour.

Mike: I once had an hour long conversation with him as to why he would not consent to an interview. It was the best unproductive conversation I ever had. The misconception was that these guys were mobsters or something making these bizarre, rough, violent movies on the sly and that couldn't be less of a fact. I think of young David and Herschell outrunning angry mobs in Wichita, Kansas in the '40s.

Lisa: They were businessmen. That's what it came down to. Obviously they chose a very unusual profession to be in, yet when it came down to it, they paid attention to what trends were happening in the industry and making relevant films that would bring in good box office. They were aware of what their fellow colleagues were up to and were often influenced by each other, even if they didn't want to admit it. There are thematic motifs and similarities between many adult films in this period, which to me is very fascinating.

She Freak is my favorite Dave Friedman movie. It's his most personal and a love letter to carny life. Some of his earlier ones like *The Defilers* and *A Smell of Honey, A Swallow of Brine* are great, but not every Friedman film is what I'd call "good".

Mike: Do you have any personal

triumphs? Any stories that you don't get to tell?

Lisa: My job is to honor the legacy of *Something Weird Video*. It's not about me. I already had a successful art career and all that. However, I have been bringing more of my own passions to the table when it comes to Something Weird since Mike's death. I started putting together record albums of soundtrack music from *SWV* films. Four years ago I released the first record album. Mike and I had discussed doing audio projects, but never had the time to pursue it. Considering that Mike used to manage punk rock bands (The Dead Kennedys and TSOL) it would've been a no-brainer for him to do this. But I had my own ideas about how the records should sound and which film soundtracks deserve to be put on vinyl. So being able to take the company in a new direction the past few years has been something I'm very proud of.

[The first album was titled] *Something Weird's Greatest Hits*. It was a labor of love and I worked on it with my pal Howie Pyro who actually collects the original records for a lot of these films. There was a group of people that I definitely asked for help because they're experts in their field and for me, it was more like I knew what I wanted it to sound like and look like. I'm pretty good at curating, which I hate that word, but I think that's one of my superhero powers. But that's it! Nothing else!

You play to your strengths. I like to organize things, so putting together the records and what I see an extension of that is gonna be *Something Weird* starting a publishing company next year. That's pretty much the direction I'm gonna go in in the future. So I would say, Mike was the one with the vision and fortunately he and I shared a lot of the same ideas about things. It was pretty easy for me to be able to continue what he did and not make things look that much different. I would say also the look of all of the catologs and video covers, that's all me. 90% me.

Mike: It's a very distinctive look. You don't mistake it for anything else. It's gorgeous. I'm sitting up now and taking notice.

Lisa: Making it as obnoxious as possible, that was my goal. Mike was a big fan of color. In fact, if he saw any white or empty spaces he was like, "Fill it up! Fill it up!" I definitely listened to him, but that was also kind of my aesthetic as well.

Mike: Is there a misperception about you or *Something Weird* that you need to clear up, or do you think everybody has a good impression?

Lisa: I think one of the biggest misperceptions is that *SWV* is a large company. Even at our biggest, we were still a relatively small company. We maybe had 8-10 employees in the heyday, especially during the VHS years when we made the tape orders in real time. *SWV* had 24-hour shifts duplicating VHS. When we switched over to DVD-R, the manufacturing time was less, so we didn't need as many employees. We were also doing Ebay for awhile. But since then things slowed down so much that we didn't need much staff at all, and now it's just me and a part-time employee (who does the DVD-R manufacturing). So I'm pretty much doing the jobs of 8 people all by myself. I even told Mike years before he passed away, "If it ever gets to the point that I'm having to do the DVD-R duplication, it's over!" Well I'm almost there now!

Sometimes customers will ask where their orders are (after placing them just a day or two before) and I have to say, "We're not Amazon! DVD-Rs are made to order!" In most cases, I can't just pull something off the shelf and send it out that same day (unless it's an Image Entertainment DVD, partner Blu-ray, or record album). Working in customer service and mail order, I've learned that you can't please everybody. But most *SWV* customers are cool.

When it comes down to it, genre film fans should be so glad that Mike Vraney spent 25 years digging up lost low-budget films and putting them on home video for us all to enjoy. I'm just grateful that I got to be a part of it all…

Go here and buy stuff: http://www.somethingweird.com/

WE'RE STILL STANDING

Ya did your best, but you can't kill the Indie spirit!

The idea was to put a call out to every indie artist we could think of and offer them free ad space. Boast about yourself, boast about someone else you admire. The catch: promote the hell out of the mag. We all win.

Those that heeded the call are presented here as they wanted to be, as eclectically and unique as they all are.

Let's get started.

So...who are WE?

HAPPY CLOUD MEDIA, LLC

We're your not-so-humble publishers and editors, over here just outside of Pittsburgh, PA. If you've played along the last twenty years, you know we started out as a film production company, formed to produce the 16mm "zombie-noir", *The Resurrection Game*, way, way back in the 20th century.

HCM, as Happy Cloud Pictures, was formed by the triumvirate of Amy Lynn Best, Bill Homan, and Mike Watt. Throughout the early '00s, we produced a number of features and shorts, were (and are) heavily involved in the indie horror industry, and were (and are) beloved by one and all.

The Resurrection Game kicked off the careers of a number of professional film workers in Pittsburgh. Numerous special effects and filmmaking students have worked on Happy Cloud movies and proved themselves to be employable by others. Carlos Savant, for instance, a key on set effects artist on *NCIS: New Orleans*, got his start on our own *A Feast of Flesh*, providing scarring, wounds, and would probably appreciate us not bringing him up every time we want to feel good about launching careers.

AMY LYNN BEST, your publisher and HCM's owner, is a classically-trained actress who produced everything that has come through our doors. As a director, captained the

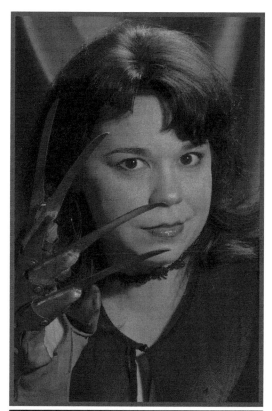

Images pages 17-18 by David Cooper.
© Happy Cloud Media, LLC.

ships for *Severe Injuries* and *Splatter Movie: The Director's Cut,* the short films *Were-Grrl, 7:45 of the Dead,* and *Zom-B-Gone*. Her starring role in *Razor Days* was met with critical acclaim, and she brought the '80s back, co-starring with legendary scream queen Brinke Stevens in Happy Cloud Pictures' *Demon Divas and the Lanes of Damnation*.

Outside of Happy Cloud, Amy co-founded Pretty-Scary.com, the first website dedicated to—and comprised of—women in the horror community, and has continued to be a vocal proponent for women in all aspects of filmmaking.

MIKE WATT, your editor and pal, has worked in nearly all aspects of filmmaking, from executive producing all the way down to processing. (For horrific details of his time working at WRS Film and Video Lab, pick up the not-wholly-fictional *Hot Splices*.)

When not filmmaking, he's writing. He wrote for all sorts of print outfits, most of them long gone now: *Femme Fatales, Cinefantastique, Fangoria* (we have just received word that Fangoria is still in print…go figure), both incarnations of *Sirens of Cinema*, not to mention *Film Threat* Online, where he was one of the more reasonable of the iconoclasts there. He's made film and film history his life's work, translating that into multiple books of film critique and history, most notably the *Movie Outlaw* series, which grew out of the lamentable *Fervid Filmmaking* (published by McFarlane Press).

DREAMHAVEN BOOKS AND COMICS

Talk about survival! Our longtime friend Greg Ketter reported that Dreamhaven survived the Minneapolis riots of May, 2020. There was damage, there was loss, and there was violence, but the store remained standing. And yet... "Just to be clear: we were nowhere near any riots/protests. The neighbors say it was four guys in a car. We were a target of opportunity. – Wendy"

We're in a wild world folks. Be kind to each other.

If you're in the area, swing by and show them your support!

2301 E 38th St, Minneapolis, MN 55406
Phone: (612) 823-6161
http://dreamhavenbooks.com

RHONDA #APPRECIATION

I liked Mike's idea for this issue—made perfect sense after the last year. As I write this, warm is the J&J vaccine that courses through my veins. I didn't hate 2020; I'm grateful for it. Sounds weird, I know. But I am weird.

Artistically, pre-pandemic I had my Patreon and my *Medium Chill* series. I had maybe two weeks between their organic ends and March 24th—the date the universe Brian Johnson-shrieked "*YOU'VE BEEN THUNDERSTRUCK!*" and then tried to kill us all. During the pandemic, I focused on teaching, not dying, and writing for my three favorite magazines: *Grindhouse Purgatory, Exploitation Nation,* and *Girls, On Film.*

I also hi-five myself for volunteering for the ID13 Project and becoming a producer. Rachelle Williams was proud of me, too. I got my name onto Full Moon's *The Gingerweed Man* (2021) [alongside *Evil Bong 666* (2017) and *Babysitter Massacre: Heavy Metal* (2020)].

But it's Dr. Rhonda Baughman I am most proud of. What a crazy bitch! She joined this online community cult and created her own courses and began a new book. The courses will launch when Baughman is damn well good and ready. Course 1 preps students to master the essay (for school returns, for work projects, or to master the essay for its own sake). Course 2 is strictly mentorship for creative writers. Course 3 assists individuals who are contemplating online instructor positions. The book is underway and remains secret squirrels for now.

ANDRAS #GRATITUDE

If there is one thing I found uplifting during quarantine, it was the podcast. This once under-appreciated art form has always been there—I have vague memories of even doing one before they were ultra-cool. As a child of *Pump Up the Volume* (1990), why wouldn't I love the podcast? I mostly listened to The Radio8Ball Show, Lydia Spin, and Casualty Friday. And then I found: The World is Wrong. A beautiful lesson that you and everything you know is so wrong, it's right, which just circles and fractals to wrong again—which is probably right.

The World is Wrong is the brainchild of actor/writer/musician Andras Jones [*A Nightmare on Elm Street 4: The Dream Master* (1988)] and writer Bryan Connolly [part of the team behind the brilliant tome *Destroy All Movies!!! The Complete Guide to Punks on Film* (2010)]. This podcast is deep and rich and…*it made me appreciate Tom Cruise*. (I appreciate his ex-wife Nicole Kidman more now, too—and Jones/Connolly cover some of her best works on the show)—but let me just say it once more. The perfect storm of re-reading Connolly, interviewing Jones and joining forces with an online witchy community led by Dr. Carolyn Elliott, I now appreciate the work of Tom Cruise. I can hardly believe it myself.

Do you know how hard it is to change my mind—about anything? I teach people how to persuade others when they write, to change reader minds with only the power of words—so it's double-plus good hard to change my mind—about anything. But change it did during the last year—and it's refreshing—filling me with tingly hope and optimism. And strangely, the urge to watch Cruise's '90s *oeuvre*. I blame you for this, Andras. Thank you.

HORROR REALM

You may actually *be reading this at Horror Realm*. This issue premiered there, anyway. At the very show mentioned below.

This is "Pittsburgh's Horror Con." It's run by talented, dedicated people who legitimately give a damn about the Pittsburgh Horror Community. They have ties to Indie filmmakers and artists, they support local theater, they're mensches. Rich Dalzotto, Michelle Linhart, and Sandy Stuhlfire. And if all the below weren't enough, there's dancing on Saturday nights. One year there was an '80s pajama party and we all got a good glimpse of what Gen-X retirement looks like.

So if you live in Pittsburgh and you miss this show because you didn't want to cross a bridge or whatever, stop whining about it on Facebook. It's here for you!

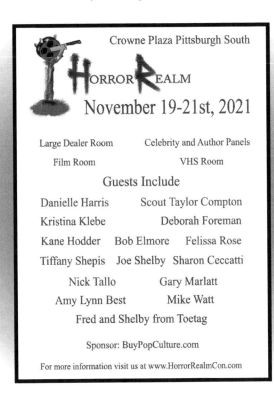

CINEMA WASTELAND

Regular readers know all about Wasteland because Wastelanders were early adopters of *Exploitation Nation*. For twenty years, Ken and Pam Kish and their dedicated crew have been putting on one of the best shows in the country.

It's not an autograph show. You aren't subjected to long lines or super-high prices. The guests generally hang and party with the attendees after hours. Alcohol is not only permitted, but encouraged ("but we *will* throw your drunk ass out if you get annoying.").

At Wasteland, everybody is family. Family you choose.

STEW MILLER

Hi there. My name is Stew Miller and this is my first time between these hallowed covers. I'm an artist, a writer, and a wizard in the kitchen. But I digress. I'm including here a few pages of a Childrens' Book I'm working on featuring MONSTERS and CREATURES and some dandy poetry. I hope you like it.

I met Mike and Amy maybe 10 years ago at the illustrious CINEMA WASTELAND in Ohio. When I first stepped into the convention on that original Friday (original for me), I was floored. The place, though not huge in square footage, was HUGE to me. The epic scope of it literally made me catch my breath in my throat and excited energy jolted through me like

Be wary alone in the tub,
or it's this creature's hide you will scrub!
They hide out in mildew and stains
and come out when you're plugging the drains
to ready yourself for a bath,
and it's then that they'll come with their wrath!
But fear not, for they're barely as big as a freckle on the head of a pig.

It looks like it's bedtime for Old Madam Lump,
Because during this time she's such an old grump.
She's wasted the daytime with knitting and games
where she tries to come up with ridiculous names
for her twenty-six cats that all live in her place
and wander around with their fluffity grace.
So let's hed to the bed oh please Madam Lump,
'Cuz your lips are all swole and your eyes are all plump.
See you tomorrow, you sleepy old git,
You'll wake up refreshed and ready to knit.

nothing I'd ever seen before. Sure, I'd been to conventions, up to and including the Chicago ComiCon, but even so (and as massive as that thing is), this was different. Why? Because this was 'MY PEOPLE'. My Horror People. They were all like me! They dressed the same, they sounded the same... they gave off the same vibes. Yeah, I was home.

But before I get too deeply into mt meetings with Mike and Amy, I want to steep back a little to when I met Douglas Waltz. Currently one of my oldest and best friends, Doug and I met in an Art Class at Kalamazoo Valley Community College in 1993. We hit it off pretty much right away. Part of it might have been my giant tackle box I was using to tote my wealth of art supplies, some of it might have been my interest in his blossoming publication of a little zine called *Divine Exploitation*, or, maybe it was our mutual love of less than stellar Horror Movies... I don't really remember, but the point is, we became fast friends. We worked together on a few of his D.E. mags, and eventually we'd start creating mini-comics which led us to something called the Kalamazoo City Comics Commission where we'd rub elbows with some fantastic local talent. We had a great time. Well, for a few years we lost contact. I got married in 1999 and had a few kids, and suddenly I found good old Douglas back in my crosshairs again. In fact, he helped land me a job at a Printing place for about a year and soon the good times were back. And it was then he'd invited me to the wild

world of Cinema Wasteland.

And so, on that first time stepping foot into C.W., a place I never would have guessed at that point that I'd be going to virtually every year sense, I was shown around by Doug. He'd been there several years up to that point and knew everyone. As one walks into the big room with all the vendors, the first table on your right is where Mike and Amy sit. You see I mention this because this is their book and I knew right then as I met him that knowing Mike, as I do now, would be one of the best things ever. In fact, knowing his wife Amy would be equal to if not slightly better than (LOL HAHAHA!) knowing Mike (she'll like that). They are wonderful people, amazing filmmakers, fantastic writers, and just a great couple of folks. But it's not them I'm here to promote. Well, any more so than I already have. I'm here to pimp Douglas. Had ya going there for a minute, didn't I?

Douglas is a writer. But he's so much more than that. He as an innate ability to laser focus on something and bring it to fruition like few others I've known. One of his wonderful pieces of literature he's recently put out is a book on THE POLONIA BROTHERS. I'm not going to front and say I knew anything more about them then just a basic knowledge of a few of their movies because I, too, frequented some little mom and pop video stores in my youth, and I rented a few of their bizarre flicks. Well, as you might have assumed, there are a TON of movies by the Polonia's, and Douglas has collected them all. This book is massive. It's overflowing with everything and anything you'd ever want to know about the Brothers. So, as a friend and as a fan, I implore you: go to Amazon, shell out the 30 bucks (it's more than worth it), and buy *Monstervision: The Films of John and Mark Polonia*. Then thank me later.

DOUG WALTZ

I write a lot.

A lot a lot.

But this is about something particular that I am extremely proud of so, there can only be one answer: *Monstervision; The Films of John and Mark Polonia*.

The majority of the book deals with fifty-five of the films that they made. There are remembrances of working with The Polonia Bros. by people who have been in their films. I managed to score two huge interviews with Jon McBride and Todd Carpenter. Two important people in the Poloniaverse.

At almost 350 pages, it is my longest thing I have written. My *Monster Killer* series of books might be close if you jammed all of the volumes into one big book.

The Polonias came on my radar when I was doing a ton of film reviews for various publications. One, in particular, *Cult Cuts*, sent me an early film, *Holla If I Kill Ya*.

I did not like it.

But more and more of their films kept getting handed to me as I am the reviewer that will watch anything and give you a fair shake.

Then I watched *Among Us* and

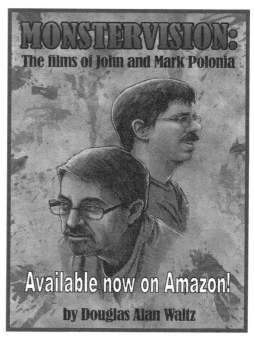

The Polonia Bros had me hooked for good. I later interviewed the brothers and Jon McBride for my 'zine, *Divine Exploitation*.

John Polonia passed away in 2008. Mark Polonia continues to make films to this day. Sometimes three or four a year. His output is staggering.

Three years ago I said I should write a book about The Polonia Bros. Here it is and you can buy it on Amazon.

NATHAN RUMLER

Part of the assignment our erstwhile editor gave us concerning self-promotion was to pick someone else to talk about for 300 words or less.

I really know a lot of talented people, so it was kind of difficult to pick just one person. Then it came to me so I would like to talk to you about one of the most fiercely creative film makers it has been my pleasure to meet: Nathan Rumler.

While he has produced and starred in many films it's his three movies that he directed that show Nathan to be one of those directors that is fearless and throws the world, warts and all in your face.

Reminds me a lot of John Waters to be honest.

Fangboner gives us a unique take on the whole alien virus/vampire genre (If that is a genre. Probably.) *Fanboner* enjoyed an actual DVD release for Wild Eye so go get it already.

Gay For Pray: The Erotic Adventures of Jesus Christ is, well it's the title. You get it. Easily offended people need not bother.

But the one that showed me that Nathan will someday be great is *Amityville Vibrator*. Between an actual magic mushroom trip being filmed to the director dropping trousers whenever a dick is necessary, and a demonically possessed vibrator, Nathan shows that he is the new head of subversive cinema.

I can't say enough nice things to say about this film. Nathan is currently remastering the film and including many extras for a Blu Ray release.

Nathan can be found on Facebook and is super nice and very friendly. I recommend going to his page now and seeing when he plans on releasing the *Amityville Vibrator* Blu Ray.

You'll be glad you did.

AT THE DEVIL'S BALL

In the beginning, Nathaniel and Sammaeal set out with one clear vision: "There's already a thousand podcasts, what's one more?" In all seriousness, what happened was they were two aging white dudes who looked out at the internet and saw a lot of aging white dudes engaging in criticism that was negative or derisive and decided to make their own that could be thoughtful, inclusive, and welcoming to fans new and old.

Starting as a solo show, Nathaniel recruited Sam to be his co-host and, despite one breakup that lasted for four hours or so, they have developed into a moderately oiled machine! Since then, they have covered over fifty films and shows that cover a wide spectrum from horror favorites to mostly lost gems, and even some talks with the folks that make indie film! Together, the guys have made some great friendships with other podcasters and filmmakers and hopefully, made some great episodes. While their listener count isn't in the millions, they are steadily growing and, regardless of audience size, they live by the code, "We'll keep doing it as long as its fun!"

To this day, and for the foreseeable future, the pair will continue their quest to provide positive, incisive and constructive commentary on horror and cult cinema with an eye or three towards making fandom a big, fun tent! And, remember, "Keep it positive, keep it constructive."

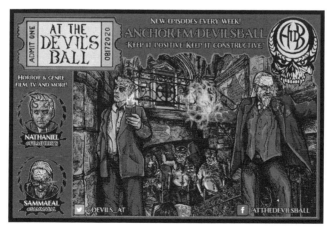

THE MUMMY AND THE MONKEY

I'm Janet Decay, Cleveland's "Yummy Mummy" and first Horror Hostess, and my co-host funky monkey man is Grimm Gorri. Together we entertain viewers on Friday night live streaming *The Mummy And The Monkey's Hairy Scary Hangout*. We stream a cheesy B- movie with added sound effects, play comedy skits that we put together, have prize drawings, and have fun with the audience live in real time. Fans can catch us on Friday nights at 9:45 pm on Facebook.com/themummyandthemonkey or watch on their big TV's through Apple TV, Roku, or Firestick. It's simple, just add Public Media Network to your smart device. We're carrying on a late night movie host tradition that spans over 50 years.

What's old can be cool again, and don't worry if the movie is bad Grimm and I will make it better!

We also have live chat shows and upload behind the scenes videos on **YouTube.com/TheMummyAndTheMonkey.**

To check out our social media links and shop official merchandise you can check out **TheMummyAndTheMonkey.com.**

Kenjji is a friend of ours who is oozing creativity through every pore. He works diligently for Public Media Network in Kalamazoo, MI (he runs *The Mummy And The Monkey's Hairy Scary Hangout Simulcast*), while also pursuing his own artistic endeavors. He has done video production, writing, and comic books to name a few.

Kenjji's FRANKIE TV Show is a clever and girly grindhouse comedy program for the gore hounds and goths. It's a great platform for indie horror filmmakers to get seen.

New episodes airing this fall on PMN(Public Media network), and a FRANKIE comic book is in pre-production.

Kenjji's latest comic book series WITCHDOCTOR is available through GRIOT Comics.

It's about Jovan Carrington, a renowned psychiatrist who vowed to give back in his community to improve mental health and social conditions. His world was flipped upside down when the spirits of his African ancestors pay him a visit with supernatural voodoo powers.

You can contact Kenjji and follow him online:

https://kenjji.com/home.html

My name is **Angel O'Connor** and I am a tattoo artist currently residing in Pittsburgh, PA. I'm not originally from Pittsburgh but moved here from Kansas City, MO. I came to Pittsburgh to pursue my career in Special Effects but fell into tattooing on accident and it turns out I love it! While Special Effects are still a huge part of my life, tattooing is my main squeeze. I've been a tattoo artist for 10 years now and will continue until I've taken over the world! Art has been a part of my life since I could pick up a pencil and I can only hope that all of my hardwork is noticed and appreciated by everyone who gets to see it.

https://empiretattooinc.com/location/pittsburgh-pa/

EXPLOIT THIS!

by Dr. Rhonda Baughman

What the world needs now is love, sweet…What the world needs now is this documentary on the exploitation film genre, actually. And love. Love is nice. But so are gleefully wicked low-budget paracinema flicks.

I fell in love with the title *Exploit This!* when it randomly (and clearly by destiny!) flew by on my Kickstarter feed. Filmmaker Eric Eichelberger [*Ghoul Scout Zombie Massacre* (2018)] knows the world needs a documentary of exquisite exploitation proportion. He's creating it for the fans! For the children! For the fans who behave like children but are well aware we need this documentary of cinema gold! And he's doing it for, I suspect, his own sense of antiquity and deep love of the artists and films who helped create the robust, quirky, and damn fine army writers, filmmakers, and actors some of us are today.[1]

I mean, come on! We're still in the midst of an epoch that I can only describe with words/phrases like: "pandemic nuttery" and "era of the great unraveling". In other words, we need this documentary and once you find out who's scheduled for the coverage, you'll need it, too.

From the Corn Fields: Director and Producer Overview: *Exploit This!* director Eric S. Eichelberger "grew up in Northwest Indiana. He got his first camera at age 8 and began making horror movies in the cornfields near his home. Eric continued to make films throughout high school which allowed him to get slightly more sophisticated with his techniques and home-grown gore effects. At the age of 18, he studied filmmaking at Columbia College in Chicago and made his first feature film, a shot on video horror/comedy called *Cannibal Teenage Riot*. Eric went on after college to work for some of his idols including Clive Barker and Stuart Gordon. He directed his second feature film, *Fear of a Limp Planet*, and his latest film to hit Amazon Prime is called *Ghoul Scout Zombie Massacre*. Eric has built a career in entertainment in post-production as well as teaching cinema."

From the Heart: "*Exploit This!* will be a feature length documentary (120 minutes) exploring the vast history of exploitation filmmaking. It will explore the development of exploitation film starting with the birth of cinema itself, to its golden age in the 1940s and 1950s, its heyday in the 1960s and

---

[1] Notice that first person, plural point-of view I tossed in there with the "us"? Not-so-sneaky writer trick, really. This doc is all Eichelberger, though.

1970s, its death and then makeover in the 1980s, and ultimately, to its revitalization in the present. *Exploit This!* will feature interviews with many the major players in the industry of exploitation filmmaking as well as major Hollywood Producers/Directors/Actors and those of what is now called 'adult cinema'. This documentary will show how low-budget cinema has shaped the independent film industry as we see it today."

From the Court of Film Royalty: Horror and exploitation film royalty for the documentary in both new and older interviews include: Herschell Gordon Lewis, David Friedman, Ted V. Mikels, Jack Hill, Roger Corman, Mary Woronov, Brinke Stevens, Larry Cohen, Rhonda Shear, Joel Reed, Debra De Liso, and Rodd Matsui.

If we're going to prance about in this brave new world and succumb to the noodle-dickings of exploitation in all its myriad forms, well then by the Tentacled Gods of Sweet Cinema History, let's make it the exploitation of a Kickstarter documentary we actually can identify with—where the exploitation is based in groovy notions of sub-par production quality, sketchy advertising, sex, drugs, violence, and many other grotesque taboo scents and sights (as opposed to, say, current economic structures exploitation of the earth and all its peoples by greedy, unrestrained capitalists). Prance, you Exploitation Kings and Queens. Prance!

Or simply check out the links below and donate to film history.

Official Site:
https://exploitthisthemovie.com

Currently over the $15,000.00 goal as of this writing!

Kickstarter:
https://www.kickstarter.com/projects/exploitthis/exploit-this-the-history-of-cult-cinema-in-america/rewards

[Suggested title]

SPEAKING CONFIDENTIALLY, OR, REFLECTING KACMARYNSKI

by **Jason Pankoke**

[Body copy]

I usually don't place myself front and center in a conversation. Even in interviews for press coverage, I tend to phrase my comments in terms of the storytellers and artists that my projects are designed to highlight as well as their potential audience gained through what I do, not necessarily my part in it. Conversely, if it can lead in organic ways to central themes and core truths in my writing and speaking, I can be my own best anecdote. I still cringe at the very thought of self-promotion.

That said, I'll stump with conviction when I need to. Creators and filmgoers in the national independent scene, as well as my friends and collaborators in the college towns of Champaign-Urbana, Illinois, know me through my attempts to explore the cinema. I published the journal *Micro-Film* for seven years until 2006, organized the Midwest-angled New Art Film Festival for a decade through 2019, and continue to write and edit the "local-zine" *C-U Confidential*, started in 2006.

And *that* said, I'm surprised that I haven't shelved it all or walked away. Managing chores and hands-on care for parents over a long distance is a haul. Doing so for four years straight

and then abruptly having to move away in order to continue is a personal seismic shift. Given the overt needs at present—clean up the house to sell, work part-time or better hours—and the semi-relief—Mom is now in assisted living, stepfather has been in a VA home—life is an unflagging stress test.

All this, and I've decided to not leave behind my C-U film studies just yet. After devoting more than 20 years to drafting a kind of chronicle that didn't exist at all for downstate Illinois, I'd rather push through with finite goals and put a proper exclamation

point on it than simply quit. Whether this is a naïve hot take or the absolute way it'll play out, I dare to continue choosing my own adventure.

I'll rely greatly on willpower and the wee hours to continue when I'm not heavy lifting elsewhere. The same can be said for many a creative we know personally. This includes my former Champaign neighbor, **Jeff Kacmarynski**, who somehow turns the DIY struggle into art with works that blend genre and stylistics from decades past. He is not well known locally or in the horror sphere as of yet, so hopefully that will change over time as he produces bigger and better work.

Dubbing them Sub-Basement Films, Kacmarynski has made a series of offbeat little shorts over the last decade. Several appear in compilations from familiar labels, like the post-apocalypse tale *Dead Therapy* in Wild Eye's *Welcome to Hell* and the dying matriarch drama *The Life of Florence Rae* in Troma's *Grindsploitation 4*. They may not sport the most polished tech specs, but they're fun to watch thanks to solid writing and agreeable twists.

Kacmarynski's next is the cosmic terror feature, *Essence*, which is being edited after more than two years of on-off production. Filmed locally on a tiny budget like the others, this one also involves talent from outside the C-U who are genre savvy such as co-star Lynn Lowry of *The Crazies* and *Shivers* fame. She and many others will contribute to the next Sub-Basement escapees, an exploitation lark titled *Witch on a Walker* and a Lovecraftian road-trip opus called *Reflecting the Void*, and I wish them great luck with future films that are poured outside the box and not in a commercial mold. Get weird, please!

Search "Jeff Kacmarynski" at microfilm-magazine.com/cublog/ *for an interview about his films, published in May 2021.*

Jason Pankoke
June 2021

[Author's bio]

Jason Pankoke lives in Illinois and has been a layout designer, copy editor, illustrator, and writer for more than 25 years. He recently contributed to two books on Quentin Tarantino, edited by Andrew J. Rausch for BearManor Press, and provided vintage video of Bruce Campbell for the Synapse Films Blu-ray release of Josh Becker's Running Time. This is his Exploitation Nation debut.

JASON McDANIEL

Filmmaker / Shadow Creek Entertainment

**https://www.facebook.com/ShadowCreekEnt
https://www.facebook.com/jmcdanielfilms
https://twitter.com/jmcdanielfilms
https://www.imdb.me/jmcdanielfilms**

I've always been a lover of films, and growing up I dreamed of being in them, or making them, I just never really thought I had the tools or the resources to do so. In 2017 I decided to attend The Scarefest in Lexington, Kentucky and had the privilege of meeting a few folks who had worked in the industry, and it inspired me. Over the next several weeks, I sat down and wrote the script to my first feature film "The Searcher". It wasn't something that I wrote to make money. I simply wanted to showcase my versatility as a writer, director, and producer. I shot the film in 16 days over the course of eight months, and finished in August of 2020. Being my first film, there are obvious flaws, primarily in lighting and sound, but I learned a tremendous amount during the process and I am proud of what

I was able to accomplish with what I had to work with. I'm looking forward to using that experience on future projects. I have at least three short films which I hope to finish in 2021, and hope to shoot another feature this year or next. The name of my production company is Shadow Creek Entertainment and
you can look for my films on our YouTube page.

I owe a large debt of gratitude to filmmaker **Tim Ritter** who was the first to suggest that I could make a film with what tools were available to a filmmaker like myself. Over the course of time he has given a tremendous amount of useful advice, and I am proud to say that he is someone I grown to call a friend. Recently he recommended me as a cameraman to filmmaker Donald Farmer, and I am beyond thrilled to work on his upcoming film "Bigfoot Exorcist". This will be the first time I will have gotten paid to work on a film set, and its something that I am truly proud of. Everyone measure success in different ways, but my goal is to someday move beyond the point of making films for a hobby and start making films as a profession; in any capacity. I highly suggest watching Tim Ritter's latest film (at the time I am writing this) *Sharks of the Corn* it is great fun and some of Tim's best work that I have seen. I also am really excited to see the release of **Donald Farmer's** *Bigfoot Exorcist*, which I am honored to be a part of, and truly grateful to Mr. Farmer for the opportunity. I look forward to working with them and other filmmakers in the future. It is a great community to be a part of.

SEAN DONOHUE / GATORBLADE FILMS

Plug 1: We have just launched our Indiegogo Campaign for *Naked Cannibal Campers Part 2: Season of the Bitch!* This is the follow up sequel to our hit last year. Check out some of our bloody perks and be a part of the action. At Gatorblade Films we always aim to deliver on the goods!

Sean Donohue
406 Stephens Rd.
Ruskin, Fl.
33570

Plug 2: As a filmmaker I have always admired Tim Ritter. *Truth or Dare, Killing Spree,* and *Creep* are some of my favorite movies he has directed. Being a Florida man, I have always looked up to him and been a fan ever since I discovered his catalog. I look forward to seeing what he puts out next and would love to work with him someday.

AND SO, BY POPULAR DEMAND:
TIM RITTER

It's hard to believe, but it's been thirty-seven years that I have been making independent video movies! My latest one is for Executive Producer Ron Bonk over at Sub Rosa Studios. He's like the modern era Roger Corman in the underground scene. He gave me a title called *Sharks of the Corn* that he thought he could sell and I ran with it. His idea was to mingle cults into it and wanted to see *sharks in cornfields attacking people. Children of the Corn* meets *Jaws*, right? And COVID-19 friendly! 90% of the movie was filmed outside, in the heat, in cornfields!

I thought about it and how much I love *Jaws*, it's my favorite film of all time! Watching extras is no longer enough, and I've seen the movie over 500 times. I *needed* to be on that set, or as close to a recreation as I could get...in *Kentucky*.

At first I was leery, then I decided to immerse myself in it [from July 2020-Jan 2021] after Ron gave me a small budget. I wanted to push things to the limit with technology and what was available. I wanted to see a shark jump up out of a cornfield and attack a helicopter! I wanted the opening scene to homage *Jaws*...in a cornfield. [Rebecca Rinehart did a spectacular job as our "Chrissy." Respect!] I wanted an adult cult of Great White Shark

worshipping members killing people. At the end, I wanted *monsters*, like say, *Humanoids from the Deep* style. Hybrid shark people! I wanted the soundtrack score to be so specific that I ended up completely composing it myself on an I-phone! And of course, all of it done seriously with a giant, comical wink.

My company, Twisted Illusions, is still at it. I teamed up again with Producer Al [*Killing Spree*] Nicolosi, 35 years after *Killing Spree*. We had "creative differences" after *Spree,* but we made up and dove into this movie, picking up right where we left off. We spent triple the budget we were provided because...*we were on fire with passion.* Loving the process, giving it our all. Ron recommended a 3-4 days shoot with the funds he provided. We filmed for 16 days! We had aerial drone shots over cornfields done by Billy Blackwell that were incredible. I used every modern trick I could think of.

My new collaborators are phenomenal. Once things are written down...the talent takes over! Lead actress Shannon Stockin is a beautiful, enticing actress with a wide range of acting talents. She also happens to do awesome practical special makeup effects under the name Michelle Macabre. Her performance is spot on and her shark bites, torn faces, and spraying blood worked like a charm. She has personally inspired me and become a muse for my work since 2018! We met on social media and she definitely enhances my creativity. I have *needed* a dedicated and really good special makeup effects artist for many years now, and Michelle is a person I can say, "Do something like Bottin's *Thing*," or whatever, and she immediately *gets it*. She had a nice resume of movie credits going when we met, and we just hit it off as horror fans and friends, doing something we are driven to do. She's also a single mom that struggles to make ends meet, and incredibly does so while never putting her creative dreams aside: acting, modeling, and effects. She deserves lots of work and success! In three years, we've already made *five* projects together!

For CGI effects, I asked my friend Dann Thombs to give it a shot, and in November 2020, holiday time for most, he immersed himself in 3-D shark models, explosions, CGI blood, and more things that elevated this little epic into near Sy Fy Channel quality with no money. Incredible. Brilliant and talented dude. I met Dann through my website and we traded movies- he's a director as well and his stuff is actually better than mine, overall, but has never seen a wide commercial release! I was blown away by his action scenes and special effects shots, so naturally, I asked him to help me, which he graciously did, on *Deadly Dares* in 2011.

And lastly, postproduction magician Larry Treadway took our 4K footage to the next level, cutting things just perfectly and adding a new dimension to it all, inspired by everything from Jess Franco to David Lynch, much like me. Like Shannon, Tread is like an extension of myself. We're good, like-minded friends, we speak the shortcut lingo, and have collaborated before on *Reconciled* and *Twisted Illusions 2*. Tread started out making movies as a young one and he and his partner George Maranville helped pioneer the horror review podcast and blog scene back in the '80s with their famous BRAINS ON FILM cable TV access show [which eventually did move to the Internet in the '90s!], and Tread is a seasoned writer, director, videographer, and graphic artist with zillions of credits. A talent that enhances my ideas when we collaborate and inspires me when I see his creations!

Sharks of the Corn ended up with a first cut of 2 hours and 9 minutes, one minute shy of the *Jaws* running time—something that I had *not* tried to do. I was hoping for 80 minutes! I had lived my dream, and it's available on limited edition Blu and national DVD and streaming summer 2021 [a shorter version]. Check it out if interested, please! And live your dreams. Life is short! Have fun and work hard doing what you love when you can, with people that you love! That is the key.

http://www.timritter.com/

TRAVIS BETZ

I make a lot of weird shit—so says my mother. I don't know where the spark originated. I do know that one day the wires in my head got bored with the traditional norms of storytelling and decided to plug themselves into the outlet that leaks that weird orangish-greenish stuff.

I've made a lot of strange films (and continue to), but my boiling desire to write a novel finally spilled over, leaving motivated burn marks in my flesh. How hard could it really be? I had a premise and a work ethic. A few months? A year tops!

CHYRON: 8 YEARS LATER

Oh... that was really hard. What started out as a simple tale about the ghost of a vampire who accidentally gets stuck inside the body of a monster hunter, evolved into a multiple viewpoint story that explores the idea (through humor and violence) that there is no such thing as monsters—just a world full of terrified creatures all hungry for a connection.
Everyday Monsters was a true birth: the seed was exciting, carrying it to term was exhausting, delivering it was painful, holding it in my hands is indescribable. I wanted to create a story that was as fun and ridiculous as it was poignant and

current. I'd love for you—sweet reader—to get yourself a copy so you might one day say to my mother, "Yes, he makes weird shit… and that's what we love about him!"

Everyday Monsters is available for purchase on Amazon in paperback and e-reader or through my website: **www.travisbetz.com**

ROSS SNYDER

Mail Order Murder: The Story of W.A.V.E. Productions

After nearly 6 years of blood, sweat, and proverbial tears since its initial conception, I'm bewildered to see my documentary *Mail Order Murder: The Story of W.A.V.E. Productions* finally arriving into the patient hands of fans around the globe. When I first befriended my co-director William Hellfire, our conversations quickly turned to the weird world of custom films and the enigmatic New Jersey based company W.A.V.E. Productions. As the director of several W.A.V.E. features and a frequent collaborator of its founder Gary Whitson, Bill had some unique insights into this subterranean world of filmmaking that I had been enthralled by since the mid '90s. As we rewatched some of the W.A.V.E. features together, we began to rediscover what a truly bizarre, singular, and vastly uncharted cinematic landscape Gary has created over the last 30 years. My initial intent was to write a book, but it was Bill who ultimately convinced me that making a documentary together about the history of W.A.V.E. would be a far better venture. We reached out to Gary for his blessing and he was kind enough to give us full access to the W.A.V.E. Productions archive including footage from the astounding, 400+ catalog of features he has directed. In May of 2017, we began our journey to locate and interview as many W.A.V.E. actors and collaborators as we could find. After whittling down over 40 hours of footage to a taut 97 minutes, I'm elated that our passion project is finally complete and has received a nationwide Blu-Ray via Vinegar Syndrome & OCN Distribution through their new Saturn's Core partner label subsidiary.

www.vinegarsyndrome.com

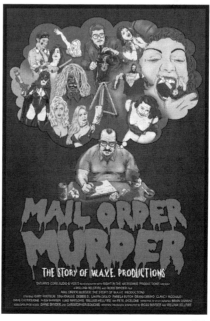

W.A.V.E. Productions

My first introduction to W.A.V.E. Productions came via my local video store in Butler, NJ. In 1995, they stocked W.A.V.E.'s original version of *Psycho Sisters* on VHS and I promptly rented it and found it quite endearing as a locally made, shot on video curiosity. A few months later, the same store purchased a copy of the *W.A.V.E.'s Most Gruesome Deaths* compilation tape and erroneously filed it in their real death / shockumentary alcove. After scanning the box and recognizing some familiar faces from *Psycho Sisters*, I rented it and watched in bewilderment as scene after scene of staged, fetishized death sequences unfolded before my eyes. While none of this content was particularly enticing to me, as a long-time lover of homegrown, SOV productions I was curious about the filmmaker behind all this madness, so I mailed away for a W.A.V.E. catalog. It was here that I learned about director Gary Whitson, his propensity for producing custom fan-scripted movies, and his unfathomably copious filmography (which at the time stemmed from only a scant 10 years of filmmaking). It was shortly after this that I first met Gary and the W.A.V.E. gang in person at the Chiller Theatre convention in East Rutherford, NJ. The W.A.V.E. Productions table was certainly an unforgettable sight to behold. A mind-bending cornucopia of crude VHS box designs, head-scratching video titles, and dense photo albums offering snapshots of scantily clad girls in various stages of peril for purchase. I continued buying W.A.V.E. movies through the mail and at Chiller shows over the years and I greatly admired the fact that Gary always stayed true to his initial focus and unceremoniously continued undaunted on his cinematic path through nearly three decades.

2021: TRAVEL PREPARED TO SURVIVE

by S. A. Bradley

I didn't ask for the anal probe. And yet, like a torch-carrying frat boy in Charlottesville, 2020 broke every consent agreement anyway...

Being creative is a struggle during the best of times and navigating a global pandemic was occasionally too overwhelming to do anything more than take shelter. My podcast, Hellbent for Horror, a narrative-driven discussion of horror films and social commentary, saw fewer completed episodes. However, all was not lost.

Hellbent for Horror was always about starting conversations and in 2020 I leaned into that. What started as solo Facebook Live broadcasts became a partnership with The Women in Horror Film Festival and robust conversations with artists and, most importantly, my listeners. It became apparent that we collectively needed this release. We needed to be seen and heard.

This kind of creativity is as ephemeral as ice sculpture, but those conversations brought new listeners to H4H, which then turned into renewed interest in my book, Screaming for Pleasure: How Horror Makes You Happy and Healthy (my proudest accomplishment).

And that begat new opportunities. In 2020, I was a guest panelist and presenter at multiple (virtual) conventions. I lectured at Webster University, where my book became part of the curriculum. The College of Idaho asked me to lecture in May of 2021 and the conventions want me back.

In 2020, I leaned into my passion for conversation when I couldn't find my creativity and I found new outlets and new friends.

ART LINKLETTER HEARTILY ENDORSES AUTHOR JAMES SABATA

There weren't many high points to 2020, but one of the great pleasures was finding the work of author/screenwriter/podcaster James Sabata. We met as guests and panelists at a convention in Arizona, (TusCon).

Sabata is a comedic horror writer, and he is the co-host of the weekly Necronomi.com podcast, where he analyzes horror films as social commentary and how horror reflects societal concerns. Since August of 2019, the show has already reached 100 episodes.

I bring this up because of all the things I admire about this the most astonishing and impressive is how prolific he is. Since 2018, James has written three full-length novels (with a fourth in proofs), two of those novels *during the pandemic*, as well as 100 episodes of a podcast.

All of that on top of being a father of four with a day job.

He didn't skip a beat.

Of course, none of that would matter is he wasn't a great storyteller. I recommend starting with his novel, *Fat Camp*. It's a slasher story where the killer stalks obese teenagers at a

weight loss camp, but it delivers so much more than you expect. It is funny and gory to be sure, but it uses slasher genre tropes to generate discussion about the hierarchy of bullies, the depth of grief, the insidiousness of self-hatred and, ultimately, the hope for change and the resiliency of spirit.

I heartily endorse *Fat Camp*!

TIM GROSS

Just like most things in my life and movies Drunken Yinzers Productions started off as a joke. It's one of those things when you are about to make a movie or write a book you cannot come up with a name to call your so-called company (insert laugh here). The idea started from a friend who quickly became my best friend (Daniel Boyd) who wanted to start writing scripts and make a movie. Daniel Boyd and I settled on the film title, *Jagoff Massacre*! I told him if he wrote the script I would help direct the movie. Never taking it too serious he finished the script quickly, we met at his house, met the two leads, a 12 pack of beer disappeared within hour of tIme, and presto (two years later), we had our first independent film made for Drunken Yinzer Productions. The response slowly built over the year or so after finishing it taking the film to conventions and showing it in theaters. Never expected anything from it but after the overwhelming response we tried a sequel unsuccessfully but moved onto entirely different project, which was a reboot of a cult like 70s film *Blood Freak*. Daniel Boyd being the writer and I doing co-director duty again was a dream come true. The film is already finding a different audience than *Jagoff Massacre* did. Knowing I co-directed two films for fun makes it all the sweeter and all it took was me finding the record button…

https://drunkenyinzersproductions.company.site/

There is a filmmaker some of yinz may have heard of or just ignored. Ignore no longer folks and embrace the future I give you a talented filmmaker like no other, **Addison Binek**! This young man has breathed not only life into the independent genre with his several projects but made me understand there is people out that are listening. It all started with his MST3K-style shorts called Movies to watch on a Rainy Afternoon where he breaks it all down for the viewer in about 13-20 minutes on his YouTube channel. From there Addison's brilliant mind knowing some of the useless information of these films that people may have forgotten put it to good use with going bigger. Mr. Binek did this format with a feature length film, *Tromasterpiece Theatre: The Battle of Love's Return*. This of course caught the eye of the legendary filmmaker Lloyd Kaufman. This open a door for this young man and made me proud as he didn't sit back to just smell the roses but continued to work on a few other projects that included Addison eventually writing and directing his own feature "Psycho Ape!" It is a funny adventure that involves a cute blonde girl's love for apes, even if it's a killer ape. To summarize Addison I believe he is a talent the world needs and when I take over Full Moon Pictures I will make him second in charge of bringing that place back from the dead! https://www.youtube.com/user/JABproducts/videos

Psycho Ape:

https://www.ebay.com/itm/333763099284?fbclid=IwAR3e4p5Rfor7U8H4SzRSCNo-mUAEYN0q0bfZEh1wQzV1_Av8Qci7hU

TOM BERDINSKI

In the spring of 2009, a mildly received but relentlessly marketed double-feature, *The Italian Zombie Movie – Parts 1 & 2* took the micro-budget indie horror community by the guts and put the young, fledgling Cult of Moi and Vous Film Producioni Company squarely on the map (somewhere...). In the years that followed, this tiny company produced the Best of 2011 Rondo Award Winning Short (*The Giant Rubber Monster Movie*) and co-produced more features including *Post Mortem, America 2021*, and *Monsters Among Men*. Meanwhile, its eccentric and promiscuous founder (Thomas Berdinski) composed soundtracks for features like *Dawn of Dracula*, *The Lashman*, *Killer Cups 3D* and *Tales from Parts Unknown*, while making (mostly) welcomed convention appearances as "Sascratch," the hero from *The Giant Rubber Monster Movie*! Ah, life was good! And then that stupid COVID thing hit and screwed everything up! But, like the obligatory sequel, we will be back...

So, get your vaccines and look for us in 2022 with new films including a long lost, shot on DV, zombie film

rescued from oblivion by the Windows 98SE certified technicians at the Cult of Moi and Vous utilizing an ancient "firewire" capture card, and a long sequel— Oops, I mean *a long-awaited sequel*—to The Giant Rubber Monster Movie featuring 15 minutes of plot and over six years worth of practical, giant monster effects!

And while you're waiting for the Cult of Moi and Vous to release more or lesser films, pick up a copy of *Psycho Ape* by our good friends **Addison Binek** (*Movies to Watch on a Rainy Afternoon*) and **Greg DeLiso** (*Hectic Knife*) for some funny, raunchy, monkey business (with a dash of Seinfeld?) Addison once said he realized any idiot could make a movie after seeing *The Italian Zombie Movie*, and now he's proved it! Our founder discovered Greg's feature, *Hectic Knife*, during a theatrical screening and immediately knew Greg had real talent (but we like him anyway...)

So, to repeat myself, and to use up the allotted word count, Greg and Addison made a hilarious film (and they even let our founder Thomas do a tiny bit of the music in it) so check out *Psycho Ape* when you are in the mood for *apesurdity* with style!

WILLIAM ADCOCK

My name is William Adcock, and I write and publish material for the *Call of Cthulhu* role-playing game, in which players take on the roles of ordinary people exploring mysteries, encountering terrifying monsters, and (often) dying horribly. A recent self-published piece that I'm particularly proud of is entitled "We Are All Savages," following a group of British soldiers and Native American scouts in pre-Revolutionary War New York as they struggle against snowstorms and illness while being hunted by a supernatural threat. The scenario combines the real world history of my home town with genuine First Nations lore, and more than a pinch of love for one of my favorite horror films to watch on a winter's evening; saying which one will give too much away. It's no stretch to say that, of everything I've written and published to date, both through community-content programs and freelancing for small-press companies, "We Are All Savages" is the most personal and contains more of who I am and where I come from than anything else, and I think the time and personal history I put into the scenario shines more brightly than in other scenarios I've written; it's available in PDF, complete with six investigative characters, at:

https://www.drivethrurpg.com/product/298233/We-Are-All-Savages

or by searching the title on Drive Thru RPG.com.

I'd like to nominate, for your attention, artist **Samson Weinberg**. Samson has a neurological condition known as sound-to-color synesthesia; this means that he sees sounds as color, and he creates digital portraits depicting what songs or voices look like when he listens to them. These pieces are beautiful, resembling swirling auroras or dazzling spacescapes (at least to my eyes), and unlike anything else you might hang on your wall. Honestly, one of the things I most want to accomplish as a writer is to produce an RPG adventure that would suit having one of Samson's paintings on the cover. Samson is also just a profoundly kind and compassionate human being, and I frequently find myself deeply thankful I've had the opportunity to get to know him and to be able to call him my friend. Without a doubt, one of the things I look forward to most with being vaccinated is being able to once more sit on his couch and see the fire in his eyes as he describes his latest project—whether that be artistic, or the plans he has in store for his backyard garden. He does most of his promotion of his work through TikTok, and videos of artwork in progress and on display can be seen on his channel @samsonweinberg. To commission a painting of your own voice (or a beloved song, etc) from him, or to buy a print, please visit his website at www.soulsoundart.com.

Editor's note: try as we might to find a piece of Samson's that would look nice reproduced here in glorious POD black-and-whiteness, but it didn't work. Check out Samson's site for yourself. It's beautiful and colorful and glorious.

DON ENGLAND

I bought a shirt from Don England. It showed Marvin the Martian taking on the Queen Alien from *Aliens*. This shirt never fails to get a thumbs up and a swift journey through security when we fly.

https://www.etsy.com/shop/dengland71?

MISTI BONDY

"Hi I'm Don's friend :) "

Misty Bondy was one of the first ones to answer the call for contributors to this issue. You REALLY have to see her gorgeous work in color. It's shamefully reproduced here.

Go here: **Mistybondy.Etsy.com and Instagram.com/mistybondy**

JASON LANE

The Art of Making the Ordinary Extraordinary or, The Reason Why I Don't Like Lydia Burris

I first met Lydia at a horror convention around 10 years ago. I was walking up and down the aisles looking at the vendor's booths when I got to an area that was thick with artists. I always bring a couple of sketchbooks to conventions, comic and fantasy shows moreso than this, so if I find an artist that I like and they

meet my financial requirements (*being poor so that I can buy their art cheaply*) I'll purchase a commission from them and maybe a print or two. After walking by some talented and nearly destitute looking artists I came across Lydia's booth and saw her sitting there, looking like she spilled out of a Neil Gaiman graphic novel with her painted leather jacket, raised red hair and crooked smile reminiscent of a certain Cheshire cat. She was running her booth with her partner David, who himself looked like a friendly vampiric version of a Crow villain and they both were talking to customers dressed similarly. I am always envious of people who hold nouveau fashion in high regard as I've always been far too cowardly to wear such wares as I've always been a minimalist in these matters. Black shirt, black pants, black vest, black boots, black do-rag, black socks, pink underwear; I'm a simple man and dress this way for both practicality and ease and, not to put too fine a point on it, because it's slimming and as an obesely obese person I'll take all the help that I can get. After watching these *Batman* villains finish their dealings I walked over and looked at her stuff.

It was good. Damn good. Amazingly good. It had touches of

Dave McKean's pencils and inks on *The Sandman* and Glenn Fabry's painted pieces but also had glimpses of John Totleben's covers from *Swamp Thing* and even Brian Froud and William Stout's works. I just stood there taking it all in at the eye when I said those words all artists love to hear.

"Oh, shit!"

She smiled at the compliment and we quickly exchanged greetings and salutations with me asking her influences and history and vendor experiences and whatnot and her showing patient bemusement over my overbearing presence. I looked over the displays of art and while there were some other very talented artists there, this artist was very, VERY talented. I asked her if she did commissions and she answered affirmatively. I gave her my sketchbook and a theme; Neil Gaiman's *The Sandman*. I paid up front (*always pay artists up front for they are almost always a poor and hungry people*) and said that I would return the next day to pick up the finished work. When I returned the next day she had not only completed the inked piece but water-colored it as well. To say I was happy was an understatement.

I immediately commissioned another painted work for a friend of mine's upcoming birthday. We talked a few more times that convention but said our goodbyes until the next

one. The mentioned commission piece arrived in the mail and it was breathtakingly gorgeous; a close up of the comic book character the Swamp Thing. I was *juuuuuuust* a little happy over this and contacted her to let her know it. She was happy that I was happy and I had thoughts of other potential art pieces running through my head all the while. The next convention that we all met each other I brought her a copy of a book that I had told her about, Neil Gaiman's *The Last Temptation of Alice*, and later that evening when a group of my hoodlum friends went out to dinner she and David joined us. All of my friends are freaks and weirdos so Lydia and David fit right in. Getting back to the hotel we sat in the lobby drinking, some moderately and myself not so moderately. And then, miracle of miracles, I had an idea.

Her painted leather coat was a wonder, looking partially weathered and partially like dragon scales glistening with blues and purples and gold. Now I myself never liked wearing something so flamboyantly cool but I did like making a fashionable statement. I usually wear leather vests and I never liked just adding patches or whatnot to it. So I asked if she would paint my vests. Paint a theme on them, actually. We settled on a price for one because 1.) I didn't want to have her overcommit or overextend herself and 2.) she may suck at doing this. Probably not but you never know. The theme was monsters; no other real definition. I did mention the word "kaiju" a couple of times but didn't specifically give her any direction other than "create what you feel". The result was a breathtaking piece that I was extremely happy with, enough so to immediately pre-commission two more; a Cthulhu themed one and one inspired by Clive Barker. The Clive Barker one is a favorite at horror conventions because it looks just amazing and it also gets me some interesting conversations.

Clive Barker fans are…different.

Lydia and I have kept in touch since then with us usually talking 2-3 times a month and always seeing each other and hanging out at conventions.

I commissioned another vest from her; the only reproduction I ever wanted. I am a big fan of Thomas Harris' *Red Dragon* ever since I read it in 1986 and have always thought that Francis Dolarhyde aka the Tooth Fairy aka the Great Red Dragon. In the book Dolarhyde is obsessed with a painting by William Blake called *The Great Red Dragon and the Woman Clothed with the Sun*. I thought it was a plot device made up by the writer but later that year in school the English teacher read a poem by William Blake. I was fascinated, as I had no idea that Blake was a real person. I went to the local library and found his painted works. Flipping through the pages of his collected arts, I saw dark religious imagery of people suffering in hell or purgatory or just in misery and then I came across it; *The Great Red Dragon and the Woman Clothed in Sun* (as it was really called). In the book *Red Dragon* there is a simple picture of the figure of the Red Dragon as pendant on the cover but the actual picture?

It was breathtaking.

This became one of my favorite pieces of art, although for (mostly) different reasons than Mr. Dolarhyde's reasons. So long story short (too late) I wanted to see if Lydia could put that image on a vest. I challenged her to do just that and guess what? She did just that. And guess what?

It was breathtaking.

It looked exactly like the original to the point where someone put the picture of the vest on Instagram where it was noticed by Brian Fuller, a writer, producer, developer, caterer (*maybe not that one*) on shows like *Star Trek: Deep Space Nine, Star Trek: Voyager, Star Trek Discovery, Heroes, Pushing Daisies*, and *American Gods* but the show he was heading at the time? *Hannibal* (available now to own on DVD and Blu Ray!). The man who was adapting *Red Dragon* to the small screen had seen Lydia's work and complimented it appropriately. I wear the vest on special occasions and meet some interesting people who also very much like the book or movies, with them sometimes quoting some small part of a dialogue. What does become worrisome is when they appear to like the book juuuuust a little too much. I just smile and nod and say "Thank you, pilgrim. I, too, am an avid fan."

That usually does the trick.

As all artists do Lydia has been experimenting with different styles and mediums always with a touch of the dark and the fantastical. She had a series of painted layered bottles that were and are incredible to behold and has dabbled in a type of architectural collagery. She also sculpted a tall completely red statue-dude that looks like a *Heavy Metal* cover and Warlock from the *New Mutants* had a baby.

It's *that* cool.

Right now she's in the middle of moving to Chicago where her works can get some more notice. She's also traveling around the United States to any places that can give her inspiration or just a cheap place to stay (Remember, artists are usually poor). You can follow her on any of the following:

facebook.com/zyphryus
Instagram: #madartistlydia
Website: http://lydiaburris.com

In closing, I need you to know that I am a very petty individual and am easy to anger or make jealous in any possible way either real or imagined. I fancied myself an artist early in my childhood but never had the talent, passion or skill to do anything with it. So seeing someone so talented and passionate and skilled do something with that ability? Well, even though I consider her a friend I still get furious, sorry, I mean jealous, just a little, over her works. But I've gotten over that, especially since I am the recipient of some fine art in the process. So check out the works of Lydia Burris. She's a damn good artist and she's getting noticed so her stuff is going to be more expensive soon but it all boils down to one thing: she's so much better than I am as an artist.

Man, but I don't like Lydia Burris.

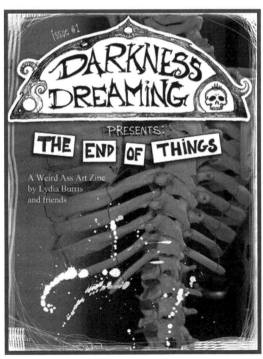

AN ACQUAINTANCE WITH IMPRESSIVE ARTIST ENDEAVORS OR: WHO KNEW SHE WAS TALENTED? SHOW OF HANDS?

by Jason Lane

A long time ago (*the early 2000s or so*)
I used to be a manager at a Hot Topic.
When I dealt with the crowds, I would have to be loud
and tell annoying teens "STOP IT."
Teens who were preppies and slobs
and stoners and snobs
and some who had absolutely no enjoyment
Some of them we'd curse
and some we'd wish worse
and some unlucky ones were offered employment.
"Pick that up!" "Fold that shirt!"
"Sweep the floor!" "Do some work!"
are some of the orders I'd yell
The customers would come in and go through
like a tornado (or two)
and make the store a living hell
There were novelty tees from '80s cartoons,
and super tall boots near our goth dressing room
and Care Bears stuffed bears stacked front to back
Our tastes were unfathomable,
we had every type of music tee imaginable
(*well, as long as it was available in black*)
There was Nirvana, Ramones,
Good Charlotte, the Stones,
and ICP set up row to row
Shirts like Vote for Pedro, The Crow
and Edgar Alan Poe
and JNCOs that could swallow you whole
Well one day we hired, a teen who desired,
for some reason to work on our staff
She seemed friendly and sweet
and was nice even to creeps
but she soon learned, "Aw, the hell with that."
Like others before she one day left our store

but a rare thing occurred sometime after years passed
I forget where I looked,
I think the kids call it Facebook?
Anyway, I DM'd her to talk about times past
Her name was Becky, by crikey,
and her temper was mighty
but we chatted about things long forgotten
How some other employees ended up
and how much Limp Bizkit sucked
and how Creed was thoroughly rotten
I stayed in touch via FB and sometimes I would see
something that she would end up making
These works were artistic endeavors
and were unexpectedly clever
and of her lack of skill I was highly mistaken
These works were woodburned and the themes were absurd;
they were different than most seen
Primitive style art is traditional and hers so untraditional.
I mean, Seriously? A dice-rolling tray with Dragonball Z?
She's made coasters with rampaging Kaiju
and even Cthulu (yoohoo!)
and the superhero scene but nothing too showy
Vikings and Star Wars and Venom and Stan Lee
and she's even had a portrait of Starman David Bowie
Her work is top notch
from bottom to top with some things that will make you say

(FORCED RHYME WARNING)
"Heavens to Betsy!"
How can you look at her works
and make with a purch?
Why, I believe that she
(FORCED RHYME ALERT)
uses Etsy.
So on your phone you should meander
and give her a stuff a gander
and maybe buy an item or thirty
She does commissions too
just as long as they're not,
er, hmmm…you know,
all gross n' pervy
Her site is GuaranteedFreshShop,
you should go there a lot and that's all I'll say about that
In closing this piece,
here's a message I'll randomly leave:
"I talked you up. Now give back my cat!"

https://www.etsy.com/shop/GuaranteedFreshShop

JEFF MONAHAN

Every once in a while you meet someone who changes the way you look at life. That happened to me when I met **Tanya Dovidovskaya**. My partners and I were looking for a casting director for a film project when she came to be interviewed. Others we'd met had experience, knew their jobs, and came with a sort of casual "hire-me-or-don't" attitude. Tanya arrived wearing a pretty white dress splashed with flowers. She spoke with an accent I didn't recognize, and told us she was from Belarus. She charmed us with her easy smile and infectious laughter. Her resume from Russia and LA was impressive. And she was honest about how much she wanted the job. Since then she's shown tireless dedication on several projects with me, no task too small or too big for her to take on. She's a world traveler and long trips we've taken together are over far too soon. A graduate of the University of Moscow, she's not only adept at her work, she's also a professional photographer, painter, pianist, violinist, and makes a mean spaghetti sauce. Once, while watching a movie late at night, we were accosted by a bat in the house. Never a dull moment. Always learning, she's pursuing opportunities to further her education in the career she loves. I laugh more when I'm with her, and smile more when I think of her. And that's sort of what life's about.

I admit it: I've never been normal. I come from a small town in Pennsylvania. Most of my family never left. And most of them worked at one, *normal* job their whole lives. And there's nothing wrong with that if that's what makes you happy. Me, I've never been satisfied with only one life. So I've been a police officer, an undercover narcotics cop, a white-collar office drone, a tour guide, a professional actor on stage, television, and in movies, a professional screenwriter, the owner of a production company, a producer and director. I don't mean to say I've been particularly good at any of these things, just that I've done them. I've also taught acting and screenwriting from NYU to CMU to Kathmandu. I didn't even know where Kathmandu was when the call came asking to go there and said yes without a second thought (it's in Nepal, between India and Tibet, and it's a marvelous place I plan on returning to soon). I was told that saying yes before I know what I'm agreeing to isn't logical. But life is to be experienced. I love to dance, cook, paint, take photos, and make art. I've written a novel and a textbook. I study Taoism and Buddhism, do yoga and meditate. I've traveled across the country and around the world, and my only regret is that I only have so many more years left to keep doing these things. I believe in peace, passion, and creating the life I want to live. One strange and wonderful moment at a time.

Jeff Monahan

---72nd St. Films, LLC---

ACTOR SCREENWRITER EDUCATOR

AEA, SAG/AFTRA
WGA
From NYU to CMU to KATHMANDU

Film, Theater, Television
Features, Shorts
Acting, Screenwriting

Contact for Information and Booking:
Website - www.72ndstfilms.com
Email--jetsm@zoominternet.net

TANYA DOVIDOVSKAYA

PRODUCER--CASTING DIRECTOR
- 'Black Lives', Documentary TV series, Producer
- 'Witnesses', Feature film, Drama; International co-production, Israel, Russia, France, Poland, Czech Republic, Belarus, Ukraine 2012-2018, Producer
- 'Actors on', TV Mini-series, 2018, Producer
- 'Perelman', Feature film, Biopic, International co-production, Russia, Bulgaria, USA, 2018, Producer
- 'Off by heart', Feature film, 2017, Producer, Casting Director
- 'Chernobyl: Zone of Exclusion', TV series, Sci-Fi, 2016-2017, Producer
- 'Frequency paranormal adventures', Documentary reality TV series, 2017, International co-production, UK, USA 2017, Producer
- 'Down the rabbit hole', Award-winning short film, 2017, Producer
- 'Onion boy', Award-winning short film, 2017, Casting Director
- 'Trans-stories', Documentary TV series, 2018, Producer
- 'The violin', Award-winning trilogy, International co-production, Israel, USA, Russia, 2016, Producer
- 'Shoes', Short film, Academy Award for 'Best Live Action Short Film' list, International co-production, 2013, Producer
- 'Bones', TV series adaptation, 2012, Casting Director
- 'Sketch.com', TV Mini-series, 2011, Producer, Casting Director
- Snog, Marry, Avoid', Reality TV show, MTV Russia, 2011 Casting Director
- 'SOS! Children!', TV-Series, 2011, Casting Director

Contact for Information and Booking:
Phone - 646.256.8806
Email - dovidovskaya@gmail.com

ROCKY ROAD TO THE CINEPOCALYPSE

by Thomas Seymour

The thing is, I've never really made any money in the Indie film industry. I've had a career in network news and even some studio and web video work at NBC Universal and IGN. My real passion has been producing and directing my own feature films. When I started in the late '90s web video hadn't matured so going to the video store and movie theaters was really the only way to discover new films. I can look back on it now nostalgically and remember how magical it seemed. I grew up in a time when digital editing was becoming possible, this allowed people like me to save up a few grand with my brother, Bruce, and friends Mike Aransky, Phil Guerette, and Tim Kulig, to make our first 16mm feature (*Everything Moves Alone*). It was a comedic-drama about a soldier who comes back to a small town to find his brother. We rented an Aaton LTR camera from the Boston Film Foundation. We shot the 90-minute feature in about ten days.

We edited on a PC with an ancient version of Adobe Premiere that crashed all of the time. Editing a feature like that was a nightmare and we essentially had to finish the film in three parts and then assemble the final version onto Beta SP tape as a master. This format was popular in newsgathering in the '90s and we could make VHS copies from there. This was a tremendous step-up from editing on two VCRs in my parents basement as I did in high school. I remember saving up my money from

working horrible fast-food industry jobs to buy a VCR from the pawnshop with a "flying erase head" to ensure my VCR-to-VCR editing would make clean cuts. You would use the "pause" button to make a cut so without the "flying erase head", trying to make edits would distort the video or cause analogue glitches. We used to shoot on an old VHS camcorder that was barely functional. I made some of my first shorts this way. *Money Run* and *Kick the Corpse* were two unwatchable action films that I made my friends and family watch. The other thing I was into at the time in high school was volunteering at the local public access station.

I grew up in a small town in central Connecticut near Hartford. Our neighborhood was a giant cul-de-sac but we would cut through to other streets from the woods at the back. One day while riding my bike in an industrial park behind my neighborhood, I discovered *Nutmeg TV*; there was literally a television station not too far from my backyard. This seemed magical; I actually knew some of the shows that were on that station. These shows were created regular people. I walked into the place and I was mesmerized. I was a huge fan of the film *UHF* with Weird Al Yankovic and so I signed up for training to volunteer immediately.

I worked on some other people's shows for a while until they let me create my own show, *Pungent Fun*. It was a terribly-made talk show. Phil hosted and I would play the keyboard. It was crass and silly; we emulated a David Letterman-type format and discussed direct-to-video action films starring Eric Roberts and Rutger Hauer that we actually really loved! Also we were huge fans of the *Toxic Avenger* cartoon and the films. The first film I ever made was on Super 8 in Junior High. It was a Claymation rip-off of the *Toxic Avenger* called *The Nuclear Warrior*. When I saw the "R" rated version of the film, I realized that Lloyd Kaufman of Troma Entertainment was doing what I wanted to do. He was like the punk rock of the film industry.

Although recently I received my M.F.A. in film production from Hunter College I initially went to Northwestern Connecticut Community Technical College to learn filmmaking. By the time I graduated I had been volunteering at Public Access, I had finished 16mm feature film (*Everything Moves Alone*) and I had an Associates degree. All this was enough to get me a "vacation relief" position at CBS News in Hartford. They were willing to hire me because of the nature of the job and also I was getting paid about 10 dollars an hour. When someone called out sick, I'd often get a call at 3:00am to come into work. You see we had to start editing at 4am to get the news on for seven or eight. CBS played large blocks of news in the morning so you'd be editing straight until noon. It was a rough job but I eventually worked my way up to full time staff editor and I was proud of that.

My film never really went anywhere; it played at the Pioneer Theater in New York and was panned by the New York Times, killing any direct-to-video deal that might have happened. The film did feature some impressive cinematography and editing and I think that helped get me hired at CBS. From there I would work for NBC Universal and even IGN. This work always felt like a day job and it always felt secondary to my filmmaking. Working in corporate media is not that different from working in fast-food or a factory. Working on other people's stuff is just never going to be as satisfying at working on your own art.

In regard to *Everything Moves Alone*, I realized maybe I was getting ahead of myself. I wasn't going to make Good Will Hunting on a $9,000 budget. Why not try to make an exploitation film? Why not try to be like Lloyd Kaufman. After all, I had worked at various video stores in my youth, perhaps I could be a direct to video filmmaker? I didn't want to give up on my dreams so I decided to make an action, sci-fi, fantasy, comedy flick called *Fountain of Death* or *Land of College Prophets* depending on what country you were in. It's a "Kitchen Sink" type of genre-blender, as Mike Watt once called it. It was about these violent college students who wake up a haunted wishing well. I think it "worked" at the time but I think it's aged pretty poorly. I tried to re-release it in recent years and people trash the film now even though it was the only film that I directed that got a "fresh" rating on *Rotten Tomatoes* at the time...I hate that site.

We had switched over the AG DVX100 to shoot *"Prophets"*. A Panasonic digital camera that shot at 24 frames per second. The look of the footage was more like film than other video cameras at the time and it was in our price range at $3000. So that's when we moved to digital. We submitted the film to several distributors. Troma liked the film and would have taken it but York Entertainment also wanted it and at the time their titles were in all the major video stores. So we went with York. They did a wide release and as a result our film was distributed in most of the major video stores like Hollywood Video and Video Gallery but not Blockbuster. I recall walking into Video Galaxy and seeing a whole shelf with *Land of College Prophets* on it. It was sold to about ten different foreign territories as well. So on the web sometimes we'd see the Russian, Italian or Spanish cover art.

It was an exciting time. I was about 24 and made my first successful direct-to-video film on a twelve-thousand dollar budget. The film sold well and we thought the distributor would be sending us checks in no time but it never came to be. That company ripped us off and as my film career slowly crept on we were never paid a dime by various distributors, some for good reason, others for nefarious ones. There was also a sobering reality. No one knew who I was as a filmmaker and no one cared even though I had a "successful" film.

Clearly I didn't understand how low I was on the food chain I was. The great recession began and although it technically ended in 2009, the effect would ripple throughout the economy for years to come. It had laid waste to many independent film production and distribution companies, also video stores that were already struggling to hold on as films began to stream more widely on Netflix.

We had upgraded to the Canon H1. It was a high definition camera that could shoot at 24fps. *London*

Our late, great friend Carmine Capobianco.

Betty for instance, was a comedy adventure that I directed (starring Daniel Von Bargen from *Malcolm in the Middle*) that was shot on that camera in 2010. It actually made it on the shelf at Blockbuster in 2012 just in time for them to go out of business a year later in 2013 ...and again we never paid a dime.

On films this small it's rarely worth it to take legal action and I think some companies know that and take advantage. Eventually we found a great company called MVD that did revenue share directly with us but by the time we made our horror film *Mark of the Beast* and released it, the video stores were on their way out and I remember finally getting the film on the shelf at Kim's Video in New York just in time for them to go out of business that following year in 2014. Even though the film starred Ellen Muth (*Dead Like Me*) and Debbie Rochon (*Toxic Avenger IV*), it never made back even a third of it's tiny budget which was less than $10K.

At that point I really think people stopped being impressed by what a filmmaker would do with no money. I had worked at a comedy website, Black20, for a few years and we even received some YouTube Award Nominations for our work back in 2008. I saw how things were changing, some of the public started to resent low-budget features. They were compared directly to studio features and considered as part of the glut of content online.

At that point my heart was broken by the film industry. I couldn't raise any more money and I was exhausted by spending years of effort and not getting anywhere. There was no ladder left to climb. It's a realization that you can make money in the industry but it's almost never actually making what you want. I truly loved filmmaking but it really felt like the industry was dying. I was so tired of being broke, believe it or not corporate media can be nomadic, some jobs just last a few years, vassals of the networks come and go for instance NBC Universal has a site called *Dotcomedy* that I made some content for and even that went under. I was living in New

York, renting a small room in Queens, most of my friends had moved on to other careers, building families. I had defined myself so much as a filmmaker that it's pathetic to say I didn't feel like I knew who I was. I took a job at the local community college, by this point I was in my late thirties.

My students really could care less about my body of work. It's not an esteem booster to work in academia believe it or not. It's a tremendous amount of work and my students want to do the work, get in and get out because they have lives to live, children to take care of and sometimes two jobs to work. I wasn't much different than them when I initially attended community college in my youth.

I didn't have an office with a window overlooking some trees. I was working out of a closet in a computer lab sandwiched between two loud active theaters in a building that used to manufacture tires. I didn't even teach as a professor until a few years ago. I was the A.V. nerd. At that point I had made eight feature films, I was middle-aged, and had very little to show for it at the time. I didn't know what I was going to do. I had a job that could pay my bills but could not keep spending my own money.

When *Mark of the Beast* first came out I started recording some footage here and there with Ken Powell, a co-worker. We would go on these VHS hunts. It was fun but we really didn't know what we would do with the footage. My new girlfriend at the time (who would eventually become my wife) took me to the Found Footage Film Festival. These two guys Joe Pickett and Nick Prueher would build a live comedy show around the VHS tapes. They had been doing this for years since 2004 and were even on David Letterman's *Late Show* showing off a famous VHS tape of a MacDonald's training video. Those guys were so funny and I loved the nostalgia I was feeling when I saw the show. I remember watching training tapes when I worked at Wendy's in high school, with a man with a golden spatula telling us how to press and flip the meat.

When Kim's Video in New York went under I went back there and took some footage on the last days. My brothers in Connecticut both worked and owned video stores back in the day. I thought I could build a documentary examining the decline of physical media and what we lost when most of the video stores went away. The promise of streaming video never replaced the revue of physical media and even though Netflix was built off the backs of independent content in the beginning, they had done away with low-budget Indie film almost all together.

This is how *VHS Massacre* and *VHS Massacre Too* came to be. I teamed up with Ken Powell and we started making the film using a Black Magic Cinema camera and a Panasonic GH4. We didn't know if anyone would care about this film. Although I had a news background I really never worked on a feature length doc. We got Debbie Rochon and Lloyd Kaufman on board along with Nick Prueher and some other folks. We had the idea to use all of the VHS tapes we had gathered and show them at the end of the film. One of the last things we shot was the Interview with Joe Bob Briggs. Joe Bob was always writing and performing but he hadn't had his own show in years. We were lucky to have caught him at that time because within a few years he had made a smash come-back with *The Last Drive-In* on Shudder.

When we went to find a distribution, I submitted to Troma cold. I literally mailed them a bluray with a letter. I had missed a chance to work with them when I was younger so they were the only company we tried. We were lucky that they actually liked the film. We signed with them immediately. The one thing I had figured out is that I can make a feature length documentary virtually for free. I could shoot an interview every month or two, gather some B-roll and build a film over a few years. No longer did I have to shoot a feature in 9-14 days like I did on all of the other films. That was always the problem with my narrative films. We were always too rushed to make the film the way we wanted. This was a revelation for me. These days most independent film companies simply do not make a profit on their titles. That's why they come and go. So there is very little meat on the bone but that is ok for me now because I'm no longer going into a ton of debt to make my movies.

When the first *VHS Massacre* was released the reviews were pretty good and people seemed to respond well to the film. The most wonderful part was that even after a few years people were talking about it. The film seemed to have legs. It even screened on MUBI a few years ago. That's like an art house film channel and I never thought I'd get the chance to be on.

A few years had gone by at this point and the hopes that streaming services like Prime and YouTube would save the Indie film industry had pretty much died. Media conglomerates owned every profitable platform and they reduced the residuals to all but nothing. They were also deleting controversial and independent films off their platform without the ability for filmmakers or even distributors to appeal. I was pissed off and I knew I needed to make a sequel. I had shied away from using the term exploitation for much of my career even though it's an advertising term "market exploitation", that really is a reference to how you market a genre title. Netflix had stopped taking exploitation films years back and with Prime and YouTube deleting these titles off their sites by the thousands. It very much seemed like the last stand of the American exploitation film. I knew what the next film was going to be about.

I hired Debbie Rochon and Ken Powell to help produce with Tim Kulig and me. I was happy to hear that Troma was interested in a sequel. That's really all I needed to know, that the film would have a home with a company that was glad to have it. Being under the Troma flag had helped solidify the film's audience. It was a victory for me. I finished *VHS Massacre Too* in 2019 and it started in the festival circuit and then Covid hit. Tim Kulig, my best friend and longtime collaborator, got the idea that we should go very heavy on the festival circuit. Our strategy was to not go too highbrow. To enter festivals that played exploitation and horror titles but to our surprise we won

73

twenty awards including Requiem Fearfest, San Francisco IndieFest, Vancouver Horror Show, WorldFest Houston and even the Telly Awards. It even played at Shudder's Mid May Massacre and HorrorHound Weekend. Even though most of this was virtual I was able to do several QandA's and panels and I think I really felt like a successful filmmaker for the first time in my career at the age of 44.

Sure, I'll probably never make a living off of my films but trying to be a good dad is really more important to me than filmmaking now. The dreams of my youth to be the next George Romero don't seem to make much sense anymore. It turns out I'm a documentary guy and not a narrative guy. Filmmakers like Eli Roth, Matt Stone, Trey Parker, and James Gunn all started off at Troma. It may be that I end up there but I think I'm fine with that. *VHS Massacre Too* will hit Blu-ray sometime this summer featuring Joe Bob Briggs, Debbie Rochon, James Rolfe, and Lloyd Kaufman.

Speaking of Lloyd. Troma Entertainment and Lloyd Kaufman to me represent the heart of the American exploitation film scene. There aren't that many giants left like him and Roger Corman. You could call them the last lions of the movement. Independent exploitation film companies can't seem to generate enough money to stay afloat long term.

Sure, Lloyd and Roger have to dabble in licensing a few of their franchises to the studio system to keep their doors open but they have to generate income somehow. There is a fear that they can never be replaced. Media conglomerates and billionaires literally start companies that impersonate Independent film companies like A24. I think Lloyd Kaufman is far more important than people realize. Exploitation films push the boundaries of taste in the form of narrative and that is an important function of a free society. Media consolidation and the erasing of exploitation films off of streaming sites without recourse threatens to sanitize cinema and culture and it's something to be worried about. It really is a freedom of speech issue. Also, shout out to the gang at *The Last Drive-In* who continue to do some amazing shows paying tribute to some wonderful exploitation films.

Troma Entertainment President and Founder, Patron Saint of Indie Cinema, Lloyd Kaufman.

SHADOWS AND LIGHT

Gary Kent is a Wastelander. He's also the real deal. As a stunt man, actor, production co-ordinator, Gary has worked from everyone from Al Adamson (*Satan's Sadists*) to Brian De Palma (*Phantom of the Paradise*). When shooting on the Spahn Ranch with Adamson and fellow stuntman Bud Cardos, Gary would run into Charlie Manson and family periodically. Bud got physical with Charlie once. Sound familiar? Like "Once Upon a Time in…" familiar? This is all in Gary's book, *Shadows and Light*.

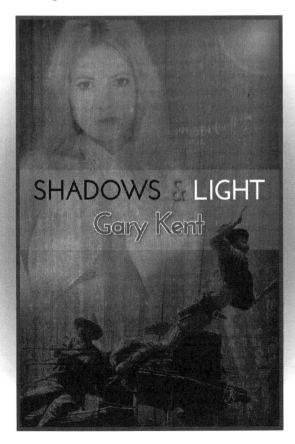

NOTLD 90: THE VERSION YOU'VE NEVER SEEN

You know who Tom Savini is. Legendary special effects artist? More or less invented the practical gore technique. Co-starred with Ed Harris in Romero's *Knightriders* after providing all the effects for the groundbreaking *Dawn of the Dead*? That guy.

Tom directed the remake of *Night of the Living Dead* in 1990, from a script by Romero. For one reason or another, *many* of his planned sequences never made it to the screen. For the first time, you can see the film as completed in Tom's head.

This is as unique a book as you're likely to find—the completed storyboards, annotated by the director, giving you a rare glimpse into the filmmaking process.

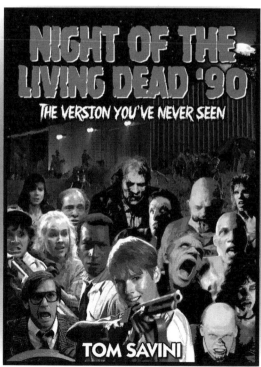

NIGHTMARE PAVILION

Andy Rausch has earned the right to call himself a writer. He's written over 50 books as of this writing. We put out one.

Nightmare Pavilion and Other Supernatural Tales collects 13 of Andy's strange, twisted, funny, and terrifying stories, including the title story, *Nightmare Pavilion*, a novelization of the cult classic horror film, *Carnival of Souls*.

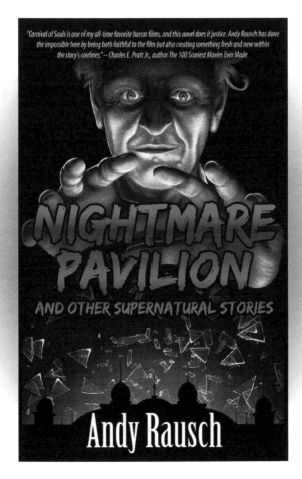

FINAL INTERVIEW

Y'all are punk rock indie horror fans, right? So you know the ToeTag crew, primarily Fred and Shelby Vogel? Lovely folk. Good to animals and children.

Fred and ToeTag got pigeon-holed for a while due to the global cult success that was the *August Underground* series. The Final Interview gets as far from *AU* as possible while still staying in the horror genre. Well, *thriller*. Anyway, check it out for yourself. **https://www.thefinalinterviewmovie.com**

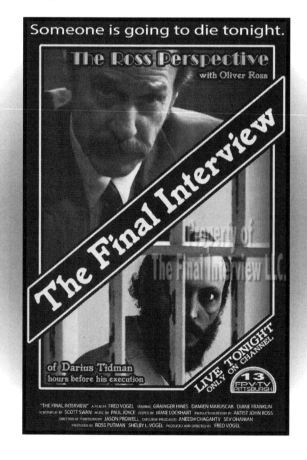

BLOODSUCKER CITY AUTHOR JIM TOWNS

*Author and Filmmaker Jim Towns is a childhood friend. He has a new book out, **Bloodsucker City**, and it sounds terrific. The plugging below comes from the book's press kit. I pulled it apart and left you with the most relevant stuff, and you're welcome.*

From Jim: "The book is set in the '30s, during the Great Depression. A young single mother named Lena comes home from work to find her young son killed, and drained of blood. The police arrest her, she's tried, and convicted of murder, and sent to Steelegate Prison for Women, a fortress-like prison built on top of an old Civil War fortress in the middle of nowhere. Only the worst of the worst are sent to Steelegate: killers and deviants of all varieties—and Lena has a life sentence to look forward to, locked up with these hard women. She slowly comes to the realization that the Wardens who run the prison are all vampires, feeding off these women one by one—women the world will never miss. When her cellmate and only friend Yvonne is killed, Lena decides she must not only escape, but also find a way to bring down this prison and its undead wardens for good.

"I wanted to set the story in 1933 because that's the year my mom was born. I grew up with her telling me stories about the Depression, and how her family lived through it. It seemed to me a time where it would be easy for someone—especially someone from an oppressed class like women were in that era—to get lost and forgotten, as our country (and the world) was preoccupied dealing with this giant crisis.

"[Now that it's out,] in 2021 I'm busy finishing post on my martial arts series *Immortal Hands*, and then I'm hopefully shooting a horror feature with my long-running collaborator Sadie Katz. Both of those projects will likely come out in 2022, along with my first chapbook of poems, writings and photographs called *Whiskey Stories*. I'm a good way towards finishing the next book already, which is also a period piece and also features an undead creature—but is a very different type of story. There's a lot of other stuff brewing as well, so it should be a busy year."

Jim, without breaking narrative, plug some other fine folk:

"So, it's a funny string of events: a good friend of mine from college, Tony Salvaggio, is part of the long-running and much-acclaimed *Castle of Horror* podcast. When *American Cryptic* came out, Jason Henderson (who runs that podcast as well as the Castle Bridge Media publishing) was kind enough to do an interview with me for the podcast. After that I contributed a story for the Castle of Horror vol. 4 anthology, and then I invited Jason onto my own podcast, *The Borgo Pass Horror Podcast*—as we're both big classic horror fans. Jason's a fantastic writer with a huge catalogue behind him. I feel we have a mutual respect and a shared appreciation for these kinds of stories. So when I was ready, I submitted the manuscript to him and it was a very rapid 'yes'. I'm very honored to have the book coming out through Castle Bridge. They've been wonderful to work with as the release gets nearer.

In closing, I'm going to leave you with Jim's Linked-In Page, because why not?

https://www.linkedin.com/in/jimtownsfilms

GAUNTLET PRESS

Many moons ago, at the very beginning of my career, I contributed a couple of articles to *Gauntlet*, an anti-censorship magazine run by author Barry Hoffman.

Years later, Barry would give me the opportunity to work with Paul Schrader, Martin Scorsese, and Robert De Niro on the *Taxi Driver: 40th Anniversary Screenplay*. Gauntlet Press puts out handsome, hardback versions of your favorite screenplays, like the Darabont book below. **https://www.gauntletpress.com/**

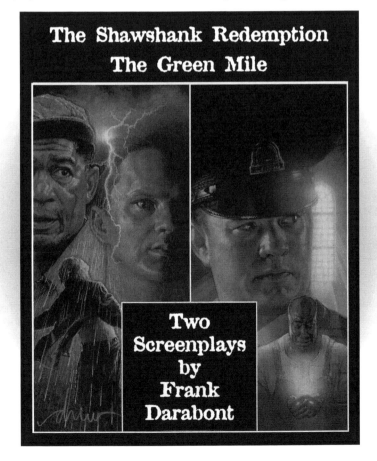

I'D BUY *THAT* FOR A DOLLAR!

by Mike Haushalter

While I used to do most of my dollar movie scavenging at second hand shops, that changed in 2020 after I saw some YouTubers talking about the big scores they were finding at Dollar Tree locations across the nation. Hoping to find some of this gold for myself I started haunting my local Dollar Tree stores to see what kind of films I could score. It was mostly slim pickings at first but around the black Friday shopping season huge boxes of films were dropped at many of my nearby stores and I found tons and tons of titles I thought would be worth taking a look at and even more amazing were the amount of Blu-rays I found.

When I began to delve into my new box of treasure I discovered that I had perhaps found too many in fact. Because as much fun as I have had doing these Dollar Tree bin dives, I seem to have ended up with a ton of duds that I just can't bring myself to review. Even titles that seemed like they would be super fun to view and review like *Clown Town*, *Demon Hunter*, *Zombie Ninjas Vs Black Ops*, *Werewolves of the Third Reich,* and *Beyond the Call to Duty-Elite Squad Vs. Zombie*s turned out to be huge disappointments (or worse) and had no good points to celebrate and so many minuses they are not even worth wasting the time or ink to talk about.

On the other hand I have made some Dollar Tree scores that were so good I turned them into Christmas presents (*Gravity* and *Road Warrior* both on Blu-ray) and I found a copy of the director's cut of *Robocop* on Blu-ray that just ended up directly on my shelf to replace the old DVD copy I had from Criterion.

Anyway here are a bunch of dollar Blu-rays that I did have fun with.

POWER KIDS (2009)

The box says: "Pint-sized Wun and his older brother live at a Muay Thai school with a few other students. Suffering from a failing heart, Wun is hospitalized and in desperate need of a transplant. A viable heart becomes available, but the donated organ is locked up in a hospital that has been overtaken by a lethal terrorist faction. With only four hours to perform the surgery, Wun's brother and best friends, armed with Thai boxing skills and determination, race to the hospital to take on the terrorists and save his life."

kids and adults. Fantastic stunt work. Some funny bits.

Minus: Slow and maudlin. Underdeveloped villains. Seemed like the children could have quite honestly been harmed while making the film.

Shelf/Bin: While it has a number of scenes that make for great YouTube content it's not that great of a film to watch all the way through or even as a party background. This one is going in the bin.

Why I risked a dollar: The box is not really all that exciting so I would have probably skipped this title if not for the fact that I had seen some crazy fight scenes from the film in one of those *WatchMojo* clips shows on YouTube and for a dollar I thought why not?

Thoughts: Who exactly was this film aimed at? It's far too violent for a family film yet at the same time a good deal of the film is lifetime channel drivel about dying poor kids. It's a real uneven mix that just didn't gel for me.

Plus: The children show a lot of skill as actors and on screen fighters. Crazy, over-the-top fight sequences between

4GOT10 (2015)

The box says: "A wounded man (Johnny Messner) wakes up in the desert surrounded by bodies, with no memory, and with three million dollars cash. On the run from a ruthless DEA agent (Dolph Lundgren), the Mexican cartel boss (Danny Trejo), and the local sheriff (Michael Paré), the more he remembers the less he wants to know about who he really is."

Why I risked a dollar: Dolph Lundgren! That's pretty much it. What more could you ask for? I mean Trejo is a plus, don't get me wrong, and I dig Vivica Fox but any action movie starring Dolph Lundgren is worth at least a buck of my money for me to give it a looksee. It's less than a rental nowadays and if I don't like it I probably will get at least a buck for it in trade.

Thoughts: Sadly the film is much more a Tarantino "inspired" crime film that's far more interested in quirky dialogue and being hipster cool than the kind of shoot 'em up action film I was looking for. Sure it has a few slow mo bullet fests to liven up the proceedings but mostly it's just strutting and posing. Not only that, I think the slow motion was just used in the gun battles to pad out the short running time more than anything else. To top it all off it's not even a Dolph Lundgren vehicle, some cat named Johnny Messner is the hero and he's not worth fifty cents let alone a dollar.

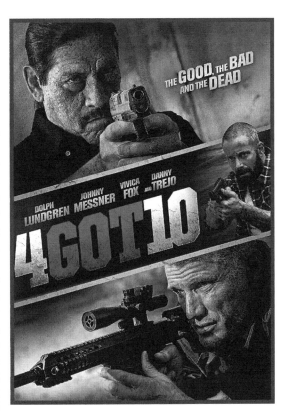

Plus: Great Surf rock/Spaghetti Western-inspired soundtrack. Fantastic tough guy cast including Dolph Lundgren, Michael Paré and Danny Trejo. Paré's sheriff gone bad is a treat and I wish he would have had more to do. Paré vs Trejo firefight. Did I mention the soundtrack? I did? Well I should have because it's really the best part of the film.

Minus: A few scenes are a bit rapey. Johnny Messner just doesn't have the charisma or star power to carry a movie and if his part was played by say Michael Jai White or Scott Adkins the film may have been more worthwhile. Surprise twists that are just a bit too expected. Dolph is mostly a no show in the action department. Film is over so fast it almost feels like they ran out of money and said yep, that's a movie.

Shelf/Bin: 4Got10 is not bad, it's a super fast moving crime thriller that never really wears out its welcome but it's not really the movie I wanted to watch nore is it one that I am gonna watch again. This one is done and in the bin.

THE JURASSIC DEAD (2017)

The box says: "A unit of mercenaries must team up with a group of tech-geek students after America is struck with an EMP attack. Deep in the desert, they find the source of the terror, a mad scientist who has also just created a living dead T-Rex dinosaur, one who turns everyone it attacks into a zombie. Now they must scramble to stay alive and save the planet from the ultimate undead predator."

Why I risked a dollar: There is a Zombie T-Rex on the cover (a Z-Rex)! This box is top tier salesmanship and is truly a display worthy bit of packaging. Zombies, dinosaurs and mercs with heavy firepower? sign me up!

Thoughts: I have been burned more than a few times by blind pick ups from Wild Eye Releasing and this was no exception. But in this case *The Jurassic Dead* is simply a bad movie, not an unwatchable one like many of the other Wild Eye releases I have suffered through. Comparably speaking, it's one of the better films I have seen from Wild Eye, in fact. It's a micro budget effort from Milko Davis (*Tsunambee, Curse of the Black Lagoon* and *Jurassic Thunder*) that borrows heavily (and unapologetically) from *Reanimater*, Tarantino films and *Mad Max Fury Road*. Dino zombies are kind of a fun idea, it's just not all that well executed one. The special effects are not all that bad so much as everything else in the film just falls a bit flat. The director and a good deal of the cast went on to make *Jurassic Thunder* which from the synopsis could have been partially made from outtakes of this film.

Plus: Great opening. Over the top old school mad scientist super villain who plays his own mood music over loudspeakers. Super juiced bootleg Mickey Roarke. *Duke Nukem* fist-fights a T-Rex. The Z rex. Good locations. T rex Trophy strapped to a Humvee. R2D2 backpack. Special effects.

Minus: Badly edited, poorly lit, ugly film. Stupid characters. Lousy Script. T-Rex size changes. Ten minutes or so of credits filler. Over reliance on green screens. The film really needed a much bigger cast, a lot more zombies, and a bigger budget.

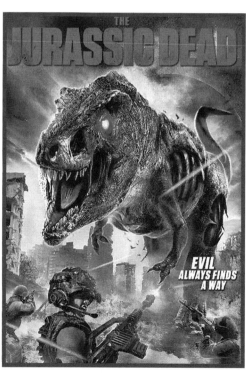

Shelf/Bin: This one is extinct and out the door. I wanted to like this one. I really did, a lot of hard work went into it and I will admit the box art alone is worth a buck for spicing up your decor.

MANDRILL (2009)

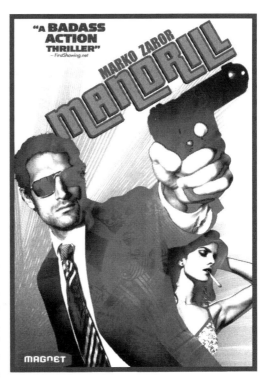

The box says: "Antonio is made an orphan when his parents are brutally murdered. As years of vengeance build up, he transforms into the relentless bounty hunter code-named "Mandrill." His sole mark is to find his parents' murderer and avenge their deaths. While on the job to capture a powerful Mafioso casino owner, Mandrill falls for his target's daughter, Dominique. As he becomes closer to her, he makes a discovery that positions Dominique as an obstacle to his ultimate revenge."

Why I risked a dollar: I love some good punch ups and I am a sucker for foreign Martial Arts outings. What can I say?

Thoughts: What a romp this turned out to be! Mandrill is a fast paced fun ode to Euro crime and pulp spy films that feels both fresh and familiar at the same time. It's a bit like the Beastie Boys Sabotage video by the way of Robert Rodriguez with lots of high flying acrobatic displays of martial arts and gun play. This was the first film I have seen directed by Ernesto Díaz Espinoza but now that I have I think I will seek out a few more.

Plus: Slam-bang trailer reel to start off the disc. Sense of humor and tons of in-jokes. James Bondish soundtrack. Colt, John Colt, and Dr. Nemesis! Plenty of on-screen fights and great choreography. Top billed Marko Zaror makes for a fine action hero in the tradition of second-tier bad asses such as Olivier Gruner, Don "The Dragon" Willson and Michael Dudikoff.

Minus: A bit corny. Bloated scenes and lethargic pacing at times. It's got an oddness to it that could alienate some viewers. A few more flashbacks than needed. Cringy, creeptastic uncle.

Shelf/Bin: This one's a keeper worth at least another view or two with some friends. It may very well wear out its welcome and be purged from my collection in a year or two but I dig it enough that I want to have it around for now.

EXTRAORDINARY MISSION (2017)

The box says: "From the director of *Infernal Affairs* comes this action-packed thriller about justice and one man willing to go to any length to get it. When police officer Lin Kai is assigned to go undercover with a notoriously ruthless drug cartel, he unwillingly becomes an addict to their incredibly potent supply. As he works to dismantle the network from the inside, his discovery of an elaborate revenge plot against his police supervisor puts his loyalties to the test."

Why I risked a dollar: From the director of *Infernal Affairs* in bold letters was the big reason and an eye catching cover. Fairly recent Hong Kong action flick for a dollar? Sign me up.

Thoughts: *Extraordinary Mission* is a mighty fine and meaty crime drama that reminded me a bit of the Johnnie To film *Drug War*. It's no way near as good as the phenomenal *Infernal Affairs* was, but since *Extraordinary Mission*'s director Alan Mak actually only co directed *Infernal Affairs* with Andrew Lau perhaps a drop in quality should be expected and truth be told until I began researching this title I didn't even know that Alan Mak even was the co director of *Infernal Affairs*. That said, Extraordinary Mission is a sprawling tale of cops vs. drug dealers full of double crosses and vendettas well worth a view to any fan of modern Asian cinema.

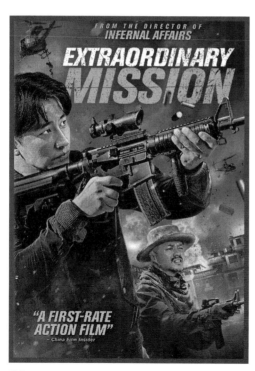

Plus: Great Score. Lots of cars doing spinning dust flying doughnuts. Top shelf characters and storytelling. It's a great looking film with high production values and epic scope. Rousing action packed stunt fueled climax. Ass over teacup car gag. Great locations.

Minus: Slow to start and drags a bit in places. Overly plotted. More drama than action. No one in the cast really pops or shines for me.

Shelf/Bin: I am gonna say this one's a keeper worth at least another view or two.

IT'S (PROBABLY) NOT A SEQUEL TO LESS THAN ZERO
REVIEW OF WILLIAM BUTLER'S *TAWDRY TALES AND CONFESSIONS FROM HORROR'S BOY NEXT DOOR*

by **Dr. Rhonda Baughman**

It's safe to say that writer/director/producer/actor/dog-lover William Butler is going for life's deluxe ultra-gulp combo value meal with extra sassy sauce. He's part *arit maat* ("offering righteous actions, living life righteously") and equal parts *Final Destination* franchise. In all cases, he's forthright, fascinating, and fucking hilarious in his new book *Tawdry Tales and Confessions From Horror's Boy Next Door*. *Tawdry Tales* is, too, like Butler I suspect—an enjoyable, gigantic tease. *Tawdry Tales* is *probably* not a sequel to Bret Easton Ellis's *Less than Zero* because THAT was *Imperial Bedrooms*; however, Butler's tell-all, behind-the-scenes of films we love, auto-bio does read at times like Ellis himself stepped in to drop some cocaine, ennui, and intrigue. That's a big compliment just in case it wasn't obvious.

Tawdry Tales delivers the goods. As the reader when not engaging in tears or laughter, I found myself dramatically reading passages aloud. Pretty sure the last time I felt like a dramatic/interpretive read was pre-pandemic, in class, and it was the day I taught some newbs about Ernest Hemingway and David J. Schow. I also spent some time with Butler's words internalizing, drawing parallels, and oddly enough -- fishing out synchronicities. Additionally, Butler covers some gaps in my knowledge about the things that *really went down* on a few movies I love and a few I love to hate. If you're reading this—then I suspect you'll want to know about these classic films, too. No spoilers here—you'll have to buy Butler's book. Frankly, it's a perfect companion to Happy Cloud Media, LLC's book *Night of the Living Dead '90: The Version You've Never Seen*[1] as well.

Butler's heart is in *Tawdry Tales'* pages: I mean, who hasn't (even quietly) acknowledged that the Universe's accompanying humanity seems sometimes to be laser-focused on ruining things like a great mood and/or one's passion for work and beloved hobbies. Seriously—things you *know* you were born to do, birthed to create, destined to… ahh, forget it because here comes DandD (Dickhead #1 and Douchebag #2) to wreak havoc, ruin mood and work and hobbies *simply because they can*. It's exhausting, as only simple-minded, petty, human cruelty

---
1 You can buy NOTLD '90 here: https://happycloudpictures.net/
Butler's book here: https://aminkpublishing.com/
-- additionally, both are on Amazon.

can be—so I would gleefully read a book where Butler seeks beautifully composed book revenge on those who behaved badly and treated others like hot garbage because they thought they were above being kind or professional. No one is perfect and Butler (and me) would be among the first to say so, BUT who hasn't therapeutically made a list of people who needed to be epically shredded for simply being raging assholes designed to harm others' dreams? I don't mean those people who "had a bad day" but those people who have made a profession out of harming others and destroying things you love because they're miserable, boring haters who get a kick out of a power play. Even the sweetest among us, come on, I know you have thought about the people who have wronged you and the chapters that could be created letting the world know precisely how awful they are—I KNOW it's not just Billy Butler and Rhonda Baughman. If it is, I'd be okay with that, too but I would also say if you've never thought about divulging the brutalities bestowed upon you by bullies, then you might be fibbing, blissfully unaware, or a candidate for sainthood. Hopefully, you're not the

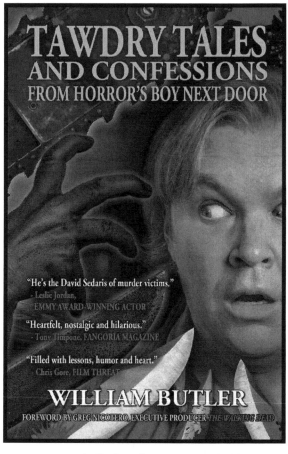

bully, but if you are people like Butler and I will write about you, purging your bullshittery, letting the world know just what a wretched poo piece you are. And yeah, maybe I do picture William Butler and I in cool clothes, walking in slow motion, a gentle wind blowing across our faces and tossing our hair about while we smile and look directly into life's camera.

Halfway through *Tawdry*, I was reminded of something else, so decided to mention it here. Once upon a time, while in pointlessly long meetings where people talked or argued just to hear themselves, if I wasn't furiously scribbling notes for my own books and stories (and also for both staying awake and making it look like I gave a damn what anyone repeatedly babbled about), then I often heard/replayed dialogue from cherished film characters to amuse myself. Those characters were there for me when needed most, like cinema buds.

Examples include Linnea Quigley's sentence from *Sorority Babes in the Slimeball Bowl-O-Rama* (1988): "That's the most stupid damn story I've ever heard."; Alvin Alexis in *Night of the Demons* (1988): "You won't get me!" (and then yes, I visualize myself somersaulting out a window); Andras Jones in *A Nightmare on Elm Street 4: The Dream Master* (1988): "It's avoid all contact day."; Marc Blucas in *Buffy the Vampire Slayer* (season 4, episode 9 *Something Blue*): "Okay, it's late… and I'm, I'm very tired now…So, I'm just gonna go far away and be… away."; finally, I often heard Butler's exasperated line in my head from *Night of the Living Dead* (1990): "Let's try and work together and get some of this damn shit done." I mention this all here, because Butler lets us know in *Tales* that he was very much like me and so many readers of this magazine: just a strange, traumatized kid who loved movies, who used them to decompress from life's overwhelming, un-fun and apparently do-this-to-survive lunacy. Movies we loved and appreciated, and probably still do, that hold innumerable scenes of characters inhabited by hard-working actors and actresses—they matter. All of those movies, the people in them, the people we watched them with or if we watched alone, and the time we spent with them, thinking of them— they mattered. They still do. They always will.

The gaps filled in *Tawdry Tales* I mentioned previously? Butler includes spicy gossip from *Ghoulies 2* (1987) and *Night of the Living Dead*, of course which makes any horror genre geek like me squee, but my God, when he touched upon the two *Return of the Living Dead* sequels (which after watching them made me want to roundhouse mannequins out of spite and wasted time/opportunity), I was not only excited, but less crabby: *Oh, I thought after reading, that's why they were pieces of shit. I should have guessed that! I'm a writer, too. Oof.* However, by the time I got to page 373, I had forgiven myself because I guessed correctly how the *Tawdry Tales* itself would end. I guessed correctly because Butler and I came to some of the same conclusions around the same time, including one of the few *really* important zingers:

People you love will die. You're going to die, too. Probably not soon, but most likely before you're ready. You won't have enough time to do everything you will have wished you'd done. Start the loving, stop overly hating, quit whining, get moving, begin making shit happen—and make it the shit that YOU want to do and have happen. It's your story—now get to living it.

You can let those knowledge nuggets annihilate you or inspire you: I prefer the latter. Finally, I do hope on Butler's continued quest, he makes another book happen: judging from his Instagram excitement about his book's Amazon ranking, I'm thinking he might drop us another hefty word gem in the future and the publishing arena would be better for it.

EVIL GRIN STUDIOS

Scott Conner was our effects lead on *Razor Days*, coming highly recommended by the great Jerry Gergely (*Babylon 5, Buffy the Vampire Slayer*, also our pyro guy on the aforementioned *RD*). Scott makes some incredible stuff, with horror and whimsy combined.

Check him out.

Made in the USA
Middletown, DE
04 August 2024

58279833R00053